IT HAPPENED IN
NEW JERSEY

It Happened In Series

IT HAPPENED IN
NEW JERSEY

Fran Capo

TWODOT®

GUILFORD, CONNECTICUT
HELENA, MONTANA
AN IMPRINT OF THE GLOBE PEQUOT PRESS

A · TWODOT® · BOOK

Library of Congress Cataloging-in-Publication Data
Capo, Fran, 1959-
    It happened in New Jersey / Fran Capo.
        p. cm. --(It happened in series)
    Includes bibliographical references (p.) and index.
    ISBN 0-7627-2358-0
    1. New Jersey--History--Anecdotes. I. Title. II. Series.

F134.6.C37 2004
974.9--dc22   2003049392

Manufactured in the United States of America
First Edition/Third Printing

Contents

Preface

I've never considered myself a historian; in fact, I did rather poorly in history class because there were always so many dates and names to remember, and since I'm a person who doesn't "remember" her age . . . well, you get the point. But after researching my first "It Happened In" book, *It Happened in New York,* I became interested in finding out little-known facts about the states—facts that make you go, "I didn't know that! How cool!" I realized that history—when told in story form—can be fascinating. So once again I began my detective work to turn up tucked-away pieces of New Jersey history to share with readers. Each research step lead me closer to the fascinating, little-known stories contained in this book, and each step involved the help of countless people who lead me in the right direction. I'd especially like to thank:

- My son, Spencer Patterson, who sat next to my desk and listened to me read every single chapter I wrote—and who would then give me his honest opinion.

- My friend and partner from *The Estrogen Files,* Anna Collins, for reading my chapters and doing an initial edit on many, even though she was busy hunting for real estate, bargains, and men.

- Charlene Patterson, my editor and friend, who once again was very easy to work with and would cheer me on with each completed chapter.

- Steve Davis, who was always enthusiastic and supportive of my work and who has heard me tell these stories over and over again to friends. Also, I'd like to thank him for insisting I include the big bang chapter.

- My mom, Rose Richards, who was telling everyone to buy the book long before the book came out.

- William Asadorian, librarian at the Central Library—Queens Borough Public Library, for once again helping me with my research, just as he did when I was working on *It Happened in New York*.

- Bobby Casulli, who told me about a magazine called *Weird New Jersey*.

- Anthony Paino, naturalist and dinosaur educator at the Philadelphia Academy of Natural Sciences, for information included in the dinosaur chapter.

- Claire Parkinson at the Register of Parks and Recreation for information on the Lenni-Lenape Indians and for leading me to historian Randy Gabrielan, who helped with the Penelope Stout story.

- Allynne Lange, curator of the Hudson River Maritime Museum, who led me to the New Netherland Museum, which helped me with information on the *Half Moon* chapter.

- William T. (Chip) Reynolds, captain of the replica ship *Half Moon* at the New Netherland Museum.

- Researcher and librarian James Lewis of the New Jersey Historical Society, who helped with several chapters and was always pleasant about it.

- The librarians at the Howard Beach Library, who said they would carry this book when it came out. I'm going to be checking, guys!

- Janet from the publicity department at Wheaton Village for faxing over all the information on the world's tallest bottle and for giving me a tour of the museum.

- Melissa Drake Campbell, manager of public relations at the Seeing Eye, for answering all my questions and for providing a two-hour, on-campus tour so I could see the operations firsthand.

- Rich, the manager and caretaker of Lucy the Elephant, who answered my questions, gave me a guided tour, and led me to the restoration architect, Margaret Westfield, who gave me a great quote for this book.

- Dawn from the history section of the Central Library—Queens Borough Public Library for running up and catching me as I came out of the rest room to say she'd found information on John Honeyman.

- Lisa Williams and Tom White of the Association of American Railroads.

- Alan Gross, friend and airship expert, who not only got me a ride on a real blimp, but also gave me firsthand information about the *Hindenburg* and the hangar. Alan is trying to get a blimp-port opened at Flushing Airport in Queens so everyone can enjoy a blimp ride.

- The staff of the *Press of Atlantic City* and the Atlantic City Free Public Library.

- Andrew Shick, director of the Passaic County Historical Society, and all the contacts he gave me: American Labor Museum, Passaic Main Library, Dey Mansion, Paterson Museum, and county historian Edward Smyk.

In the Beginning
· 65 Million B.C. ·

About 200 million years ago, dinosaurs of all shapes and sizes roamed the hills and valleys of Earth. But it was one very special duckbill dinosaur that roamed the conifer forests along the coast of what is now Pennsylvania, a *Hadrosaurus foulkii,* that would change the course of scientific history.

This particular *Hadrosaurus foulkii* lived around 65 million B.C. He weighed four tons, was about 30 feet long from the tip of his nose to the tip of his tail, and was as tall as a two-story building. In life, this dinosaur, although big, was not particularly ferocious. He was more like a large, placid cow; a plant eater that browsed leaves and branches along the marshes and shrub land of the Atlantic Coast. Considered part of the duckbill family because of its birdlike jaw and skull structure, this type of dinosaur lived and traveled in herds, and the females laid eggs in nests and nurtured offspring for a long period of time.

The *Hadrosaurus foulkii* enjoyed lolling around in the water a good distance from shore. Unfortunately, one day he got a little too bold and headed out into fast-moving water and was swept into the current. He drowned, and his limp body floated out to sea. The body came to rest below about 100 feet of seawater and was soon covered in mud and sediment.

As the water level dropped and the flesh decayed, the bones absorbed the minerals and seabed sediments, allowing them to be preserved as an intact skeleton—intact except for the head, which has never been found. The rest of the bones were discovered during a dinner party millions of year later.

Farmer John Estaugh Hopkins owned a gorgeous mansion named Birdwood in Haddonfield, New Jersey, on land that had been underwater millions of years before. The water had long-since receded, and the sediments had turned into marl, a crumbly nutrient-rich soil often used in fertilizer. Hopkins liked to invite vacationing guests to his estate for dinner. One summer night in 1858 his guest was William Parker Foulke, a scientist and fossil hobbyist who owned a summer house next door. On this particular evening Hopkins mentioned that his farm diggers had found strange bones twenty years earlier in a Cretaceous marl pit near the rear of his house. Foulke's interest was piqued, and he asked his host if any of these dug-up bones remained. Hopkins told him they had been given away to friends as souvenirs, and supposedly some were even being used as doorstops and window jams.

Foulke persuaded Hopkins to allow him to reexcavate the old pit where the bones had been found. They walked down to check out the site, but in the intervening twenty years, the marl pit had become choked with overgrowth and eroded debris from a nearby pond. Eventually they called in one of the original diggers to help them locate the place where the bones had been found, but his memory wasn't sharp. After a few minutes of scratching his head, he picked the wrong site.

Fortunately, the *Hadrosaurus* wanted to be found. On the second day of digging, the original marl pit was discovered. Foulke and fellow academician Dr. John H. Slack watched as dirt was shoveled out. About 10 feet below the surface of a ravine leading to a rivulet locally known as Cooper's Creek, they found a large jumble of black bones laden with iron deposits. Foulke's hair stood on end! Up from the pit came a hipbone, nearly all of the fore and hind legs, twenty-eight vertebrae, a lower jaw fragment, and nine teeth. Foulke then had the bones carefully transported three-quarters of a mile to his residence in a straw-filled cart.

Sensing a discovery of grave importance, Foulke carefully sketched, measured, placed on a board, and wrapped in cloth every bone—and even the shark teeth—found in the pit. Once the bones were secure in his home, he called in Dr. Joseph Leidy, a member of the Philadelphia Academy of Natural Sciences and the country's foremost vertebrate paleontologist at the time. Leidy was known as the world's smartest man and possessed encyclopedic knowledge of the natural world. He was the first person in America to use the microscope as a tool in forensic medicine.

Leidy immediately knew the significance of the find—this was the first reasonably complete dinosaur skeleton ever found in the world! It was the first real proof that dinosaurs had existed. Until this find the very idea that gigantic reptile species could have existed was highly controversial. People believed the scattered fossil fish and teeth found under the ground were leftovers from the great flood described in the Bible, even though the teeth were a hundred times the size of those belonging to any animal they'd ever seen.

Only seventeen years before the discovery of the *Hadrosaurus,* Dr. Richard Owens, a close friend of Queen Victoria, a world-renowned authority on anatomy, and the founder of paleontology in England, had coined the word "dinosaur" from a combination of Greek words meaning "terrible lizard." In a report he published, Owens suggested that the strange large bones periodically found were from members of a reptile family that had died out in some past age. Nothing else about these mysterious creatures was known because not enough bones from any one animal had ever been found.

By 1853 some dinosaur models had been created in England by Owens and a sculptor named Benjamin Waterhouse Hawkins. But the models were based on nothing more than speculation resulting from a few collected bones and were essentially formless, serpentine strings of vertebrae topped with crocodile-like skulls. This new discovery in a marl pit in

Haddonfield, New Jersey, was a truly amazing find for the world!

Leidy identified and labeled each specimen. He made the first sketches of the creature based on careful study of the skeleton. And he reached a conclusion never before heard of in the paleontology world: This creature was bipedal—it stood on two feet! Leidy wrote, "The great disproportion of the size between the fore and back parts of the skeleton of *Hadrosaurus* lead me to suspect that this giant extinct herbivorous lizard may have been in the habit of browsing, sustaining itself kangaroo-like in an erect position on its back and extremities and tail."

Leidy insisted the digging continue, and it did through October, with diggers shin-deep in gray slime, but little else was found. Leidy was the one to name the dinosaur *Hadrosaurus foulkii.* Some say *Hadrosaurus* was in honor of the town in which the skeleton was found, Haddenfield, but others say it comes from a Latin word meaning "heavy stout lizard." Foulkii honored the scientist who had found the intact dinosaur, William Foulke.

On December 14, 1858, Leidy formally announced the startling data to the scientific community. The information hit like a lightning bolt, causing a rift in the community because Leidy's findings were so different from those of Owens. But sculptor Hawkins, who had worked with Owens, saw the importance of the find and offered to mount the *Hadrosaurus* skeleton for the Philadelphia Academy of Natural Sciences for no charge. Since many bones, including the skull, were never found, Hawkins had to improvise. He used the skull of a modern iguana as a model for the original display. (The skull has since been corrected.) The mount was completed on November 21, 1868, and immediately created a worldwide sensation. People could now glimpse a creature from millions of years ago!

Hawkins was asked to build replica mounts in Washington, D.C., and New York City. However, his New York exhibit was terminated after a gang of thugs sent in by Boss Tweed, New York City's corrupt Democratic Party boss, and his ring of greedy politicians destroyed Hawkins's partially completed models with sledgehammers and then buried the fragments in a park. The ring saw the exhibit as an unnecessary expense from which they would derive no profit, so they put an end to it in their own special way.

A few years later the real bones had to be replaced by plaster bones because the air was causing them to erode, a condition known as pyrite disease. The bones were put back in their original wooden storage boxes, along with the specimen cards handwritten by Leidy himself, and are today catalogued as exhibit ANSP 10005 for others to study.

The site of the discovery remained unmarked for 126 years until an ambitious thirteen-year-old Boy Scout named Christopher Brees decided to research the location. He found it in an unofficial garbage dump and obtained permission to clean and mark the site's location in 1984. In 1994 it became a National Historic Landmark. Today visitors can follow the crude paths to the tangled ravine and visit the discovery site of the first dinosaur to rock the modern world.

The Missing Weeks of the *Half Moon*
· 1609 ·

Henry Hudson, the famed English explorer, sailed four expeditions between 1607 and 1611. Two were aboard the *Hopewell,* and the other two were aboard the *Half Moon* and the *Discovery*. While Hudson was a methodical, meticulous planner and determined navigator, he was not a good leader or judge of character, and he never quite reached his goal of discovering a northwest passage. However, he managed to make a significant contribution to the history of New Jersey.

Hudson's first voyage on the *Hopewell* was to find a passage to the Far East by way of the North Pole for easier trade with China and Japan. He didn't succeed because his route was blocked by ice, but he got closer to the North Pole than any other sailors of his time. On his second voyage aboard the *Hopewell,* the exact same thing happened. In the fall of 1608, the Dutch East India Company invited Hudson to Amsterdam to discuss a business proposition—that he lead a voyage sponsored by them to discover a northwestern passage around the north side of Novaya Zemlya, an island near the Arctic above Russia. Undiscouraged by his earlier attempts, Hudson was game to try once again.

For this third journey he was given a 60-foot-long flat-bottomed boat—the kind that Dutch fishermen used in shallow waters. His orders were to set sail aboard the *Half Moon* on

April 1, 1609, from Holland. He chose eighteen Dutch and English sailors for his crew. One of the men chosen was Robert Juet of Limehouse, England, and that's where the trouble began. Juet was a born seaman and good at his trade. On Hudson's second voyage he had been first mate, but they had a dispute that led to Juet's gathering the crew in near mutiny. Hudson had vowed he would never again hire Juet, but he begged forgiveness and Hudson gave in because Juet was an able seaman. When the *Half Moon* left Amsterdam on April 4, 1609, with Captain Hudson at the wheel, Juet was a ship's officer. Juet kept a detailed journal, and some speculate he used the journal to plot revenge against Hudson for the incidents on the previous voyage.

About a month into the voyage, as they passed the west coast of Norway and headed toward icy waters by the tip of North Cape, the Dutch sailors, used to warmer seas, began to complain about the cold weather and icy conditions. Since half the crew spoke Dutch and half spoke English, they couldn't understand each other, further adding to the tension. Fights broke out. Still, Hudson was determined to forge ahead. His obsession with finding a passage made him ignore the complaints of the men.

Seeing this as his chance to get the crew on his side, Juet related a story to the men of a Captain Barents and his crew who had wintered on the harsh, icy islands that lay ahead. He told of how the captain as well as most of the crew had died. Then he turned to the already angered men and shrewdly asked, "What man among you is eager to give his life merely to prove snow and ice may kill you?" None were willing, and it is believed that Juet then led the crew in mutiny, refusing to do their jobs until Hudson turned the ship around. (Juet made no journal entries from May 5 to 19, the time of the supposed mutiny. The surviving account of this time comes from Emanuel Van Meteren in his *Histroie der Nederlanden,* published in 1614.)

Another side of the story suggests that Hudson believed there was no Northwest Passage, and upon hearing the complaints and threats of mutiny, seeing the ice, and wanting to try a different route, he conveniently decided to "disobey orders" and turn the ship around. He had recently resupplied and had ample provisions to explore elsewhere. Regardless of the reason, Henry Hudson and crew headed for North America.

After the turnaround, Juet again began making entries in his journal. The *Half Moon* traveled to the coast of Virginia and tried to find a narrow passage that might lead from the East Coast to the Pacific Ocean. As they traveled up what is today called the Jersey Shore, Juet made notes about what he saw, consequently producing the first written record of New Jersey. Though Juet might have been a troublemaker, he had a way with a pen and wrote in a September 2 entry, "This is very good land to fall in with, and a pleasant land to see." This quote has been used many times in New Jersey literature.

Juet also noted "broken ilands" that lie between today's Atlantic City and Little Egg Inlet. Describing what is now known as Barngat Bay and its inlet, he wrote, "a great lake of water, as wee could judge it to bee . . . which was in length ten leagues. The mouth of that lake hath many shoalds, and the sea breaketh upon them as it is cast out of the mouth of it." The *Half Moon* continued around Sandy Hook, where the men went into the bay to fish and get fresh water.

In an entry on September 4, Juet described the crew's first encounter with natives: "The people of the Country came aboard of us, seeming very glad of our coming, and brought green tobacco, and gave us of it for knives and beads. They go in deer skins loose, well dressed. They have yellow copper. They desire clothes and are very civil."

On the very next day, however, he wrote that the crew "durst not trust them." After several trading sessions with the Indians and some nighttime ventures onto Jersey soil, disaster struck. On September 6 some crew members shot at the

Indians, and one of the crewmen, John Colman, was killed when an arrow pierced his throat. He was the first white man killed at Sandy Hook. Two Indians were killed as revenge, a precursor to future trouble.

On October 2 Hudson decided it was time to head back to Holland to avoid further trouble with the natives. As they were pulling away from shore, Juet noted that he saw "a cliffe, that looked the colour of white green, as though it was either a copper or silver myne." He was most likely describing the serpentine rock of Hoboken.

Worried about getting punished for mutiny or treason, the crew insisted Hudson sail to the shores of England instead of to Amsterdam. They arrived on November 7, 1609.

Interestingly, Juet somehow managed to sweet-talk Hudson and again sailed with him on his fourth and final voyage in the spring of 1610, this time aboard the ship *Discovery,* once again on a mission to find a passage to China. True to his unsavory ways, Juet again led a mutiny. The mutinous crew put Henry Hudson, his son, and eight other men overboard in a rowboat somewhere near Canada and left them adrift. They were never seen again.

As for Juet, he died before the *Discovery* reached shore, taking to his watery grave the secret of the reasons behind his missing journal entries. In some ways he served his captain well, for his mutiny caused Hudson to discover the New Jersey shoreline and consequently the Hudson River, which is named after him.

To this day, New Jersey celebrates Hudson's discovery, and the New Jersey Historical Society has Robert Juet's bound journal entries from April 4 to November 7, 1609, in its archives. A few times a year, a *Half Moon* replica ship and crew reenact Hudson's journey along the Jersey Shore as described in the original ship's log.

The Mother of Middletown

·1645·

This voyage seemed like so many others before it. A group of settlers from Holland were heading toward New Amsterdam (present-day New York) to start a new life. But the sea had other plans for them. The calm ocean waters started to stir as the sky above them darkened. Waves crashed, and a violent storm threw the ship off course. The vessel crashed into the shore of Sandy Hook.

Though shaken by the rough voyage, all of the passengers arrived unharmed—but their worries were not over. They had landed on hostile Indian ground and were in danger of being attacked before they reached the protection of the New Amsterdam settlement.

Among this group was a young couple, Penelope Van Princes and her husband, whose name is unknown. Her husband had been sick onboard the ship, and the wreck had not helped his condition. He was too weak to travel to New Amsterdam. The other settlers, worried for their lives, were not willing to wait until he regained his strength. Penelope had a decision to make. She could leave with the others and save her own life or stay with her sick husband and hope the Indians wouldn't find them before he recovered and was ready to travel. She decided to stay. The rest of the group scurried off, promising as they waved good-bye to send help once they arrived in New Amsterdam.

Trying to be brave, Penelope comforted her husband and attended to his needs as best she could. Unfortunately for them both, a few hours after everyone departed, a band of Lenape Indians came trotting down their well-worn path called the Minisink Trail (today's Kings Highway) and discovered Penelope and her husband huddled together.

Penelope watched in horror as the Indians easily slaughtered her sick husband. When they turned on her, she fled, but they were quickly on her with their tomahawks. They slashed her abdomen, mangled her arm, and fractured her skull before she fell down bleeding and unconscious. There she lay as the Indians admired their handiwork, confident she was dead. They then built a fire, cooked themselves a comfortable meal in celebration, and went on their way, satisfied that they had eliminated these intruders.

But Penelope was not dead. She lay still until her attackers were long gone. When she felt she could muster some strength, she managed to slowly and painfully inch her way away from the beach to the edge of the woods to hide. She found a hollow tree and crawled into it. There she huddled like a frightened child until nightfall.

In the darkness she crawled to the embers of the fire that the Indians had left. With determination and an incredible will to survive, she managed to get a small blaze going. She slept by it, soaking in its warmth all night.

The following morning, having mustered a little more strength, Penelope went back to the tree to hide. The tree was her lifeline. She used the inside as a hidden shelter, while she ate the gum and fungus on the outside for food and drank the dew from the leaves for water. From her hiding spot she could see the body of her dead husband on the beach. Frightened and weak, she had to stay out of sight of the Indians until the rescue party arrived from New Amsterdam.

After a few hours of being cramped in the tree, thirst made her wander out a bit to find more water. As she was crawling, two Indians popped out of the woods. Everyone was startled and froze in their tracks. The Indians were surprised to see this wounded white woman crawling towards the beach. They menacingly stood above her. Penelope looked up in horror, suspecting this was the end of her and wishing she had been killed with her husband. As she made ready for the tomahawks to render the fatal blow, a miracle occurred. To her surprise, the Indians started to quarrel. Apparently the younger one wanted to finish her on the spot, but the older one wanted to make her a prisoner at their camp. The older man won, and the wounded Penelope was swooped up like a slain deer, flung over his shoulder, and carried miles back to their village.

At the village, an Indian woman nursed Penelope back to health. For the next few years, she lived among the women and children, long having given up the desire to escape. She felt safe with the Indians.

The story doesn't end there. Although the Indians and white settlers were at odds, they did trade with each other, and eventually word got out that a white woman was being held "prisoner" at an Indian camp. The settlers believed it to be the same woman they had left long ago at the beach at Sandy Hook. They sent in representatives who demanded her release. After some negotiations, none of which involved Penelope, they decided to let the woman determine her own fate.

Penelope had mixed feelings since these Indians had treated her kindly, while the settlers had left her to die. But in the end she decided to return to her own kind. She wound up marrying a man named Richard Stout in 1648 and having two children. Stout was an influential man. He and five other Dutch families founded the village in New Jersey that would become known as Middletown. Penelope and the old Indian who rescued her remained friends and visited often.

One night Penelope's old friend risked his life to tell her that the Indians were growing tired of all the new settlers living close by and infringing on their land and were planning a midnight attack. The old Indian had hidden a canoe for her to take to New Amsterdam to escape from the massacre. Penelope told her husband, but he didn't believe that the now-friendly Indians would rise up against them. He ignored her pleas to escape and went back to work.

Penelope, still having scars from the wrath of previous warriors, escaped with her small children by canoe to New Amsterdam. When Stout saw that Penelope had fled, he decided that maybe there was something to this rumor and gathered and armed the townsfolk just in case.

At midnight, when the Indians sounded the whooping cry, the townsfolk were ready. But instead of shooting, Stout and companions boldly approached the Indians and attempted to reason with them. They said they would fight to the death with their guns to protect their women and children, or the Indians and the whites could call this whole thing off and continue to live in peace. The Indians, unused to such a confrontation at the beginning of an attack, weighed the options and decided to sign a peace treaty with Stout. The next day the settlers agreed to buy the land on which they built Middletown, and a protection system was established for both whites and Indians. The treaty was mutually observed.

The Stout family became very prominent in town. Penelope's abdomen must have healed because she ultimately gave birth to seven sons and five daughters. Some of them moved on and established the town of Hopewell in 1715, founding a Baptist church there as well as many others in Middletown. The Stouts grew in number, and in the eighty-eight years from the birth of her first child, Penelope's descendants are said to have multiplied to 502. Reasonably so, Penelope became known as the "Mother of Middletown." Reliable sources say that she lived to be 110 years old.

The Thirteenth Child of Mother Leeds

·1735·

One dark, stormy night, on a lonely stretch of road called Scotts Landing in Leeds Point, Atlantic County, deep in the Pinelands of South Jersey, an event occurred that would forever haunt and terrorize the people of the Garden State.

Jane Leeds was struggling to bring a child into the world. Her husband, Daniel, was an oysterman who worked the inlets and marshlands of Leeds Point to make a meager living. With twelve children already crammed into their small home, Mother Leeds felt she was cursed with this thirteenth child.

As the time of delivery drew nearer, a midwife and several of the elderly neighborhood women were called in to assist. They all appeared nervous as they waited by the flickering glow of the candle for the child to be born. Maybe it was the thunderstorm outside, with lightning ripping through the sky and crashes of thunder sounding like bombs, that made them nervous. Or maybe it was the fact that Mother Leeds was said to be a witch who had a liaison with the Devil himself. Whatever it was, there was an eerie tension in the air, unlike during the birth of any other child.

As Mother Leeds tossed and turned in agony, as many a mother has in childbirth, wishing for the child to be born, she yelled, "I don't want anymore children! I wish this child be born a devil!" The other women looked at each other as chills went down their spines.

Within minutes after the mother's cry, a healthy baby boy was born. Everyone sighed in relief. The women wrapped the baby in a homemade blanket, and mother and child smiled at each other.

Then suddenly the baby began to change. His face started to melt like molten wax and became distorted. The sound of cracking bones was heard as the baby's face turned into a horse's snout. Then the body began to stretch, and batlike wings sprouted from the shoulders. The body grew longer and longer and stretched into the shape of a humped serpent. Razor-sharp claws sprouted from the hands, hooves sprouted from the feet, and finally a long, heavy forked tail completed this demon child.

Everyone watched in horror and disbelief. Then the thing let out its first blood-curdling cry as smoke flared out its nostrils and it raised its head toward the ceiling. With the birth cry sounded, it turned its head, and its red eyes glared at the women. They knew they were in trouble. In an instant it was whipping its tail around the room, beating the women without mercy. Finally it turned on its mother, cursing her for cursing him. Satisfied with the bloody damage it had caused, it let out one last cry and flew up the chimney into the night, thus beginning its reign of terror in the neighborhood.

And so the demon legend was born.

This is the most widely accepted tale of the New Jersey Devil, the most famous of New Jersey legends and the official state demon, appointed so by the New Jersey legislature in 1939. New Jersey is the only state to have an official demon.

Since Mother Leeds wasn't taking notes at the time of this child's birth, there is no official record of what actually happened on that fateful night in 1735. Some accounts claim the demon child made its first meal out of two of its siblings; others say it was really just a deformed child who was shunned and locked in an attic, and then rumors spread. Still other accounts say Jane Leeds had a fight with a local priest who cursed the child. The descendants of the Leeds family say the Jersey Devil was conceived by the Shourds family of Leeds Point, the owners of the house in which the baby was born. The Shourdses insist the Leedses were responsible for bringing the creature into the world. Like Rosemary's baby, this is one son that no mother wants to own up to.

A final version of the story suggests that a Pinelands hermit lived in isolation as part of a deal with the Devil. In exchange for protection from the beast, he had to feed it and avoid contact with any human beings.

Whatever its birthright, tales of the creature spread panic throughout the Pinelands—so much so that it is alleged that the demon was exorcised from the area in 1740. But apparently exorcisms have a statute of limitations, since this one was only good for one hundred years of banishment. Sightings of the creature returned on cue in 1840 and were recorded as far away as New York and Philadelphia.

But the true Devil's lair is in the Pinelands. That's where the sightings began, by people in the area sometimes referred to as "Pineys," who called the creature the Leeds Devil. They held, and still hold, a solid belief and deep-rooted fear in the demon's existence.

There have been several thousand sightings since 1840. The New Jersey Devil has been blamed for everything from taking dead cattle, to spooking horses, to tearing apart German shepherds, to failed crops, to massive chicken slaughter. Many skeptics pass the stories off as sheer fantasy, and some say it was merely a crazed sandhill crane.

Prominent individuals throughout the years have sworn they have sighted or had bouts with a hellish-looking creature, even in broad daylight. One such notable was Joseph Bonaparte, Napoleon's brother, and the former King of Spain (who hid out in New Jersey for a while). Joseph was said to have spotted the beast while hunting on his estate near Bordentown in the early 1800s. Another respected eyewitness in the 1800s was naval hero Commodore Stephen Decatur, who went to the Hanover Iron Works to make sure that the cannonballs being made there were the right size and shape for the attacks against the Barbary pirates. While he was lining up a shot on the firing range to test the equipment, in full view and in broad daylight he saw the Devil flying across the target area. With a steady, cool shot, Decatur blasted a hole through the demon. But like any fiery devil does, it simply ignored the wound and went on its demonic way. Those who knew Decatur said he was a respected military man, and if he was lying, it was the only lie he ever told.

The most fascinating batch of Jersey Devil sightings occurred during January 1909, when thousands of residents from thirty different towns in the Delaware Valley area claimed to have seen the evil fiend.

It started on the morning of January 17 when a Mr. E. W. Minister, the postmaster of Bristol, Pennsylvania, awoke at two in the morning. He looked out his window and saw a creature with a ram's head, long thin wings, and stubby legs. It emitted a cry that "was a combination of a squawk and a whistle . . . beginning very high and piercing and ending low and hoarse," as the *Daily Republican* of Bucks County reported.

The next day a policeman in Burlington, New Jersey, sighted what he called a "jabberwock" with no teeth, eyes like blazing coals, and "other terrifying attributes." Newspapers all around the country began reporting the sightings. Mass hysteria followed.

Strange hoofprints were found on roofs and in backyards. Some folks claimed they were chased up trees by the Devil. Others saw the bloody face of the creature up close and personal. A dog in Camden was attacked, and the owner reported fending off the beast with a broom. Hunters organized dog posses to try to track down the culprit, but the hunting dogs were too scared to follow the tracks.

Reports came pouring into police stations. Schools closed,

and people locked themselves in their houses. The papers dubbed it "the most notorious visitation ever" of the Jersey Devil. A whole fire department was called in on one occasion to shoot a powerful stream of water at a strange creature perched on a roof in West Collingswood. The beast swooped down, and the fire crew ran for cover. Many articles were printed in the now-defunct *Philadelphia Record* chronicling the Devil's exploits.

By January 22, 1909, mills had closed down in Hainesport and Gloucester County. The demon started making visits to eastern Pennsylvania, and the Philadelphia Zoo offered a $10,000 reward for the creature's capture. All throughout the Pinelands people were in a panic. Norman Jeffries, a publicity hound and theatrical booking agent, and his friend Jacob Hope seized this opportunity. According to the *New York Times,* "[Jeffries] purchased a kangaroo from a traveling circus . . . and painted weird symbols on the animal's head, chest and back and then announced to the world that he had captured the Jersey Devil after a terrific fight in the woods." For added effect, they glued claws and wings to it and claimed it was an Australian vampire.

People believed the Jersey Devil had been captured. But after a few months, the sightings started again. This time they ended when police found a stuffed bear paw attached to a stick and a sign that read THE JERSEY DEVIL IS A HOAX. Since 1951 neither the police nor the press have responded to reports of Jersey Devil sightings.

Many times it has been reported that the Jersey Devil has been slain, but, like Elvis, sightings of the creature continue to this day. For those who still believe, there are various Web sites with pictures and firsthand accounts of encounters with the Jersey Devil.

One group, appropriately called the New Jersey Devil Hunters, has gone so far as to start a crusade to prove the legend is true. This group is comprised of several devoted individuals in their twenties with diversified skills, from expert tracking abilities to extensive knowledge of the Devil's antics. Although they have never met the Devil face to face, they feel they have enough artifacts and strange footprints to prove the demon exists.

Whatever the actual story, the Jersey Devil has been immortalized in lore, is feared by generations of adults and children, has had a professional hockey team named after it, and has appeared on the silver screen in a film called *The 13th Child: Legend of the Jersey Devil.*

While the foundation of the Shrouds house, where the Devil and the legend were born, can still be found 200 yards off Scotts Landing Road, skeptics scoff at the tale, but, fact or fiction, to date no one has ever proven the Jersey Devil doesn't exist.

Top Spy for
Washington
· 1776 ·

They say you never really know who your neighbors are, and in this case it was the ultimate in double identity. At 1008 Canal Road in Griggstown, off a side street near Bunker Hill Road, hidden behind a patch of tall trees and shrubs lies a small white one-story house with blue shutters. During the Revolutionary War it was the home of a man named John Honeyman, who neighbors thought was a true Loyalist. But, in truth, Honeyman was one of New Jersey's best-kept secrets, the James Bond of his time, a Patriot and spy who reported directly to the big man himself, none other than George Washington.

John Honeyman was a Scotch-Irishman who was born in Armagh, Ireland, in 1729, the son of poor Scottish farmers. He had little formal education and was a farmer until he was forced to become a soldier and fight for the British in the French and Indian War. He was tall, strong, and active. He wound up on the same Canada-bound boat, the frigate *Boyrie,* as a Colonel James Wolfe. While on the boat, the colonel slipped down some stairs and would have broken his neck had Honeyman not acted quickly and caught him, thus saving his life. In appreciation Wolfe made him his bodyguard, ordering Honeyman to be with him at all times.

During the great attack on Quebec, it was Honeyman who safely rowed Wolfe to the other side of the river, but when they landed Wolfe was shot. Honeyman carried him to a shelter where he died. Honeyman was given an honorable discharge from the army, along with several praise-filled letters that Wolfe had written about him. When the war was over, he traveled to America.

He married a girl in Philadelphia, and when the Revolutionary War broke out, he managed to get an interview with General George Washington due to the letters Wolfe had written about him. Washington was impressed. They had several more meetings.

Honeyman moved to Griggstown, rented a house, and settled in. Soon he was having regular meetings with Washington, and it is believed that it was during this time that they made a contract for Honeyman to become a spy for the American side.

The best thing a commander-in-chief can have during any war is knowledge of what the enemy is doing and the state of its military. Honeyman was to become the man who gave Washington this information, the master communicator of information. Only Washington, Honeyman, and his wife would know his true identity.

Washington and Honeyman set up an elaborate scheme that could rival the plot of any Hollywood movie. Since Honeyman had been a British soldier, it would be very easy to convince people his sentiments went with the Tories (those who supported the British). The plan was for Honeyman to let it be known that he was a Tory and to befriend the British soldiers. As soon as he thought it was safe, he was to leave his family and "fall in with the British army," posing as a butcher who supplied provisions. This cover gave him access into and out of the British camps, and while posing as a butcher, he could roam the country in search of cattle and get the lay of the land without arousing suspicion. He was to stay with the British until he gathered enough information to help Washington's army. Then he was to wander close to the American lines and get himself "caught" so he could come before Washington and pass on the information.

Washington promised that when he heard Honeyman was near the American lines, he'd send word offering a reward for his arrest but only if "the notorious British spy" was captured alive and brought back unhurt to him.

During the month of November 1776, Honeyman befriended the British. He discovered that the British forces in Trenton were not disciplined. It was winter, and it was cold; the soldiers were idle, and their guard was down. Since he knew the habits of British soldiers, having been one himself, he knew that come the holidays they would get even more carefree. He studied the lay of the land in Trenton and made a mental map that he would be able to pass on to General Washington. Anything that he thought could help the Americans he noted.

Washington desperately needed the information Honeyman was collecting. His ragged army had been ousted from New York, narrowly escaping complete destruction. By the first week of December, he had been chased clear across the state of New Jersey and was now forced to retreat across the Delaware River into Pennsylvania. He knew he was on borrowed time. If he didn't get some information quick, the British would simply wait for the river to freeze, then walk over from Trenton and finish his army off. Worse, most of his enlisted men's terms of service expired on December 31. In a letter to his brother he wrote, "I think the game is pretty near up."

Determined to go down fighting, Washington came up with the only plan he could: He would cross the Delaware River in the dark of night with his ill-equipped forces and attack the army of Hessians (top-of-the-line military men employed by the British) waiting on the other side. In order to make the plan a success, he needed a lot of information: the best time to launch a surprise attack, the exact number of troops in the British camps, if they were building boats, if they had secured the town. In short, he needed information that only John Honeyman could supply. The fate of the American army and the future of the country was in his hands.

Honeyman, like any spy, was playing a dangerous game. If the Tories found out that he was a spy, the British forces would immediately be informed and he would be killed. But his acting skills were perfect: No one on either side suspected this forty-six-year-old butcher.

On the morning of December 23, Honeyman felt it was time to tell Washington what he knew. He purposely went near the American lines on the New Jersey side, pretending to be just a Tory butcher out to gather supplies for the day. With a rope in one hand and a whip in the other, Honeyman approached a cow lingering by a fence. He made himself rather conspicuous, pretending he was engrossed in his work. He wanted to be caught, but he couldn't make it look that way.

He scanned the area for American soldiers. Then he spotted two cavalrymen sitting behind the bushes beside their horses. He purposely walked closer. When the men spotted him, they yelled "Halt!" But what kind of acting would that have been if he'd stopped? He had to let them chase him. He ran as fast as he could to "escape." The two soldiers jumped on their horses and quickly caught up with him. But Honeyman continued the act by putting up a fight, keeping them at bay with his whip.

Normally the soldiers would have simply shot him. But once he told them his name, they knew they had caught themselves the grand prize, the most wanted man on Washington's list. Honeyman put on a good show. They had to straddle him and put a pistol to his head before they could tie him up. They knew they had to bring this "British spy" back alive and unharmed as per Washington's proclamation. The two soldiers managed to bind his arms and bring him across the river to Washington's camp.

At the camp the two soldiers grinned triumphantly and shoved the spy through the door. Washington was waiting for him. He congratulated the men on their fine work. Honeyman continued his performance by pretending to be frightened in front of Washington. The soldiers snickered. Honeyman stooped his broad shoulders. His hands were bound tightly behind his back, and he had the look of a man about to be hung. In front of the soldiers, Washington berated Honeyman and threatened him with hanging. Washington then turned to the two men and sternly told them to leave the room so he could interrogate the prisoner. As soon as the guards left, Washington and Honeyman smiled at each other.

Honeyman quickly told Washington everything he knew, giving details on where the British were stationed in Trenton, how many soldiers there were, what equipment they had—everything that his keen powers of observation could remember. He reported there were no signs of boat building so they weren't equipped to cross the river and come at Washington—they were probably waiting for the river to freeze so they could walk across it and get him. They hadn't fortified the town. Honeyman also said the Hessians were planning a big celebration for Christmas night in Trenton.

It was just the information Washington needed to plan his daring attack. He was eternally grateful to Honeyman. He considered him one of the most valuable men in his army, and he was going to use every means to protect him for a job well done.

About half an hour later, Washington called the guards back in and told them to take the prisoner to a log cabin that served as their military jail. The cabin had one window and one door. The guards were told to watch Honeyman overnight and that in the morning he would face court martial. "If he tries to escape, shoot him," Washington ordered. Honeyman was dragged to the cabin, given supper, then locked inside. The guards stood watch outside.

In the middle of the night, a mysterious fire broke out in the haystack near the guardhouse, and the guards left to put it out. Using a concealed key Washington had given him, Honeyman slipped out of the cabin. A shot rang out, but he got away. He conveniently "found" a horse and then later ditched it and crossed the icy river, wading part of the way. Nearly frozen, he ran to the nearest Hessian outpost in Trenton and was brought to Colonel Rall's headquarters. After telling Rall the tale of his capture and that he was to be shot at dawn, he convinced the colonel that he did not tell Washington's army anything that would jeopardize the British. Rall, seeing this tattered, frozen, and bruised man, believed him.

Rall pressed Honeyman for information on the condition of Washington's army. Honeyman painted a dreary picture, telling Rall that the few men that were left in Washington's army were dying of starvation and freezing to death. He told him the men were on the verge of mutiny. It was music to Rall's ears. Completely confident, he decided to continue with plans for the big Christmas celebration and let the rebels self-destruct.

The stage was now set. On Christmas night, 1776, while the Hessians drank and partied, Washington and his tattered army of 2,400 men silently crossed the ice-choked waters of the Delaware to a point 9 miles above Trenton. A Tory farmer had somehow gotten wind of the impending attack and tried to warn Rall, but he was busy playing cards and wouldn't be disturbed. Desperate, the farmer scrawled a note for him, but Rall put it in his pocket unread.

Washington's army defeated the surprised, hungover Hessians in less than an hour, killing over a hundred of their most fearsome fighters, thus changing the tide of the Revolution.

As for Honeyman, he snuck away to join another British troop in New Brunswick, knowing that if he was in Trenton at the time of Washington's invasion, it would be hard for Washington to save his life. When the news spread of Washington's victory in New Jersey, the name Honeyman was not mentioned so that he could continue to spy for Washington until the end of the war.

When Honeyman's neighbors heard of his escape, an angry mob, led by John Baird, descended on his home one night and shouted for Honeyman to come out. But only Honeyman's wife and children were inside. With all four children cowering in the corner, the brave Mrs. Honeyman stepped onto the porch and faced the seething mob. "We know he's in there. If he doesn't come out, we'll burn the house down!" She tried to assure them he was not inside, saying they could search the place if they wanted, but no one took her up on her offer. Not knowing what else to do, she ran inside and quickly returned with a piece of paper in her hand. "Who is in charge here?," she asked. Baird stepped forward. She then handed him a letter dated November 6, 1776. Baird read it out loud to the angry throng. The curious crowd was taken aback.

> To the good people of New Jersey, and all others whom it may concern. It is hereby ordered that the wife of John Honeyman, of Griggstown, the notorious spy, now within the British lines, and probably acting the part of a spy, shall be and are hereby protected from all harm and annoyance from every quarter until further orders. But this furnishes no protection to Honeyman himself.

It was handwritten and signed "George Washington. Commander-in-chief."

The dynamic duo had thought of everything. After a brief discussion, the confused crowd left grumbling. Mary Honeyman sighed in relief.

John Honeyman was arrested twice more, charged with treason, and released. After the war was over, Washington did not forget him. He publicly told people of Honeyman's brave endeavors while posing as a butcher and personally visited him at his home. The town that once had hated him and shunned his wife now embraced them. He was revealed as a hero who had risked his life for American liberty.

There are no records that Honeyman was ever paid for his daring services, but maybe that too was kept secret. Historians believe Washington compensated him well. Honeyman prospered and had seven children. He lived to the ripe old age of ninety-five.

Until recently there was no monument commemorating John Honeyman's patriotism. He only had a modest headstone in the Lamington Church Cemetery in New Jersey, among the graves of dozens of other soldiers of his era. But on May 26, 2002, that all changed. One hundred and eighty years after being laid to rest, the unsung hero of the American Revolution finally got his due with a rededication ceremony and gun salute.

As John Baird, the man who once led an angry mob to Honeyman's home, said after the war, "John Honeyman did more for the cause than many who are shining heroes today."

The Rich Ghosts of Morristown

· 1788 ·

The year was 1788, just seven years after the Revolutionary War ended, and ghosts, instead of cannons, were causing quite a disturbance in Morristown.

About 20 miles outside of Morristown there was a wild, desolate region known as Schooler's Mountain (today known as Schooley's Mountain). Ever since the local citizens could remember, there had been stories of buried pirate treasure on the mountain. The treasure was protected by the spirits of savage pirates, and no one dared anger the likes of Blackbeard and associates—until two brave men decided to go after some of the loot.

These two nameless men believed in the existence of the treasure and wanted it. They also believed in the ghost legend and decided that in order to get to the treasure, they should first speak to the spirits of the pirates. Since neither of the men had experience in talking to the dead, they decided to enlist the services of a man who did. This man was Ransford Rogers, a Connecticut schoolmaster who was often heard saying that he was not afraid of spirits and, in fact, was able to talk with them and they with him. He also had the ability to send them away at will. This was the man the treasure-seekers wanted on their side. So in August of that year, they journeyed to Connecticut to talk to Rogers.

Hearing their offer, Rogers saw his chance to make a quick buck and create a whole new business that he felt would be much more challenging and profitable than teaching. But he was smart enough to know he couldn't be obvious in his plans. He agreed to come to Morristown and help these two men, with the understanding that he first had to attend to what he loved most, his teaching. Rogers did a little research and found that he could take charge of a small school just outside of Morristown. So by September, with his alibi in place, he was set to take the two men on a wild ghost chase.

The two men contracted Rogers to do whatever was within his power to induce the spirits to reveal the location of the buried treasure on the mountain. Rogers explained to the men that the spirits couldn't be rushed, which gave him the needed time to observe the people of Morristown to see how easily they could be fooled. To his satisfaction, with the right devices, he felt that they would be an easy target.

Being a learned man, Rogers was quite knowledgeable in chemistry and the art of persuasion. Like any good con artist, he knew what he had to do to totally convince these people he was legit. The next part of his plan was to find as many treasure-seekers as possible.

He gathered forty men—men who believed in his integrity and honesty and who were greedy for the loot. With all the men in place, Rogers realized he needed an accomplice to carry out his dastardly scheme. So who better to trust than a fellow schoolmaster? Rogers went back to Connecticut and laid out his scheme. The fellow schoolmaster was eager and ready to participate.

The stage was set for some ghostly happenings. Rogers arranged nightly meetings in dark, lonely places like empty fields and the outskirts of the forest. To ensure secrecy, he told the men to keep any witnesses away.

Prior to the meetings Rogers would use his alchemy skills to set up mines to explode during the secret midnight rendezvous. These explosions served as proof that he was indeed communicating with the spirits of dead pirates. For enhanced effect, a couple of loud knocks, strange voices, and other sounds (all coming from the other teacher) were produced to invoke terror among the forty believers. During the last meeting an apparition appeared in the trees.

Rogers and partner had these guys going for a long time with their award-winning performances. During one meeting Rogers had all the men lie face down with a sheet of paper held out in their hands, telling them the spirits would write the directions to the treasure on the papers. Then he collected the papers, carefully slipped one with writing on it into the pile, shuffled them, and lo and behold, instructions on what they were to do next was on one of the sheets!

Among the instructions was a demand from the pirates. According to Rogers, the pirate spirits felt that in order to trust the men with their treasure, the men first had to prove their sincerity and worth. Each man was told to pay the spirits the sum of twelve pounds in gold or silver (not the traceable New Jersey paper loan money that couldn't be used outside the state). They were to hand the money to Rogers, who would act as the spirits' agent. After all, he was their communication device, and without him none of this would be possible. When all forty men had paid, they would be led to the treasure. It was now November 1788.

Not wanting to be the one to spoil the reward for the group, or to be left out, each man set out to get the requested money. Not one person questioned this! Most of them were uneducated country folk, and some even put mortgages on their farms and sold their cattle. They each figured the money would come back to them tenfold, with the blessings of the pirates. Only a few of them couldn't raise the money, but the benevolent and shrewd Rogers let them slide, assuring them the spirits knew they had tried their hardest.

It was winter by the time all the money had been collected.

There was no way they could start the digging in the bitter cold, so the spirits told them that on the first of May the expedition would begin. The treasure-seekers anxiously waited.

They all gathered at midnight on May 1, 1789. However, the air was still cold, and they sensed something was terribly wrong. Great explosions and fireworks occurred, and at the edge of the forest appeared a very angry, indignant ghost who stomped its feet and then vanished. Rogers calmed the terrified men and then ran off to see what could be angering the ghosts. It must have been a stellar performance, for not one of the forty men dared go after Rogers or the ghost.

When Rogers came back, he shook his head like a garage mechanic does when he's about to tell a customer his car needs a whole new engine. He told the men the pirate spirits thought that someone in the group had betrayed the secret of their prior meetings during their winter hiatus. The ghosts refused to tell the whereabouts of the treasure until someone confessed. All the men vehemently denied any betrayal.

They were sent home to do some soul-searching and to wait and see if the ghosts could be calmed. Once again, they all obeyed, and not one of them suspected the scamming schoolmaster.

Not satisfied with the money collected, or with having this group of men's total faith, Rogers felt the need to push the envelope. He gathered a second group of five men and collected money from them as well. But two groups still weren't enough. With a hunger for more money, and while he had the other groups on hold, he set out for the richer sect in Morristown.

Donned in a white sheet and using a "superficial machine" (some kind of tin can) to alter his voice, Rogers made a ghostly call upon a well-respected, affluent churchgoer in good standing. His spirit appeared and told the man of how he too might obtain the riches that lie beneath the soil on Schooler's Mountain. The fine gentleman, never before having had the pleasure of meeting with an apparition, believed it to be one and was interested in what the ghost had to say.

He carefully followed the spirit's instructions and gathered a group of rich men interested in becoming even more wealthy, who began attending those same nightly meetings that the other groups had been put through. As promised in return for the secrets of the treasure, the new members also paid a fee to the honorable and gifted spiritual worker, Mr. Rogers, who would, of course, in turn remit the payment to the spirits. No one bothered to question Rogers's integrity or why spirits would need money.

This new group was made up of educated men, and Rogers knew he had to use more sophisticated magic than was required for the common folk. One of the antics he pulled was collecting some fine bone dust, which he assured the rich third group was the dust of the pirate spirits who held the secret to the treasure. Each man was given some bone dust to serve as a magic charm to keep the spirits from harming them. And, as always, Rogers told them this was to be kept in the strictest of confidence, lest they meet the fate of the first group and anger the spirits.

That night the men all left with their charms. One absent-minded fellow left his bone dust in his pocket. His wife found it and demanded an explanation. The man tried everything to get out of it, but the wife persisted, accusing him of witchcraft and being in liaison with the Devil. Not wanting his wife to fear him, he told her of the treasure, the ghosts, and Mr. Rogers.

The wife, still afraid that her husband had been lured by the Devil, told her friends. Soon everyone had heard of the secret meetings. Rogers, fearing the jig was up, hired two more ghosts to make appearances to reassure his believers that the treasure would soon be revealed and to not believe those trying to discredit him.

Desperately trying to save his master plan, Rogers, with the courage of a few libations, went to one of his rich followers dressed as a ghost and gave him some instructions. This time, however, with the seed of doubt already planted and the liquor making Rogers's ghost sound rather strange, the man became suspicious.

The next morning, after the ghost was long gone (just in case it was real), the man decided to look around his property. Sure enough, he found some horse tracks that lead straight to the house of Mr. Rogers.

The police got involved, and through investigation it became clear that Rogers had executed a well-laid-out plan. However, old beliefs die hard, and one man bailed Rogers out of jail. Rogers was quick to skip bail, but he was arrested again and this time confessed that none of it had been real.

With his confession in place, all that was left was to try him in court. But somehow Rogers managed to escape from custody, skip town with all the money, and was never seen in New Jersey again.

In 1792 a pamphlet, "The Morristown Ghost," was published, telling the entire story of Mr. Rogers's escapades up until the time of his disappearance.

Who knows, maybe he did have a spirit friend or two that helped him slip by, invisible to the law, or maybe there was still a believer remaining that helped him get away.

Let the Leaders Duke It Out

· 1804 ·

People have often asked during a war, "Why don't they just let the leaders duke it out?" Well, that's exactly what happened on a fateful day, July 11, 1804, in Weehawken.

Aaron Burr and Alexander Hamilton had a stormy political relationship. They were contemporaries who had fought in the American Revolution, and like most people on opposite political sides, they had quite a few nasty things to say about each other.

Alexander Hamilton was born in the British West Indies in January of 1755; thirteen months later, in Newark, Aaron Burr entered the world. Both served under General George Washington. Hamilton became an aide-de-camp, and Burr served on Washington's staff during the war until he was transferred after antagonizing the general.

After serving their country in uniform, both men decided to toss their hats into the political arena after the Constitution took effect in 1788. Both were handsome, quick-witted, and intelligent and had defined personalities and similar aspirations.

Hamilton became the first secretary of the treasury under Washington from 1789 to 1795 and was the chief author of *The Federalist Papers,* which advocated a strong central government made up of wealthy men. He also established the Bank of the United States. Burr became a New York senator in 1784 and was appointed attorney general of New York in 1789. He was a member of the Republican Party.

Things started to steam up as the two men got deeper into politics. Almost every schoolchild's history book mentions their disputes and the famous duel. But what many people, even the well-read, don't know is that the hatred between the two was mostly caused by an act of deception that Burr orchestrated and ultimately used to break the grip that Hamilton and his Federalist cronies had on the supply of investment capital in New York.

In a nutshell, Hamilton and the Federalists controlled the capital monies in New York and who they were lent to by controlling the Bank of the United States. Whoever controlled the capital in essence controlled the government of the state because borrowing money was vital to the establishment and growth of new business. Adding to this was the fact that at the time voting was restricted to free white men who owned property. If you couldn't get money from the banks, you had no money with which to purchase property and therefore didn't have a right to vote. The Federalists, with Hamilton in the lead, shut out the small business merchants and artisans who, in turn, supported the Republicans.

Burr wanted to change all this. Often short on cash himself, he wanted to open a private bank that would loan money to the working class. But in order to do this, he'd have to get a loan from a big bank and probably end up paying exorbitant interest rates. He was in a catch-22 situation.

Then, in 1798, yellow fever struck New York and parts of New Jersey. A committee headed by Dr. Joseph Browne (who happened to be Burr's brother-in-law) was formed to provide clean drinking water in the hope of curing the spread of the disease. Burr saw this as his golden opportunity. He strategically formed a board of directors made up of three Republicans and, after much persuasion, three Federalists, of which

Hamilton was the most prominent. (Yes, Burr did some smooth-talking and convinced his political enemy to join the committee in the name of this public-health crisis.) In order to put his plan into action, Burr needed this unified front of Republicans and Federalists to pass a proposal that allowed his newly formed water company to be a private company as opposed to a government-run company that would be out of his control. Hamilton, wanting to do what he could to eradicate the fever, wrote a testimonial letter that persuaded the committee to grant the proposal and make Burr's water company a private one.

But before the proposal was granted, Burr made his secret move that ultimately garnered the wrath of all Federalists, especially Hamilton. Burr made some last-minute alterations to the legislation: He changed the amount that the water company could raise from $1 million to $2 million and then added a clause that would allow the company to use surplus capital to purchase public or private stock. No one noticed the changes. With the law passed, the newly formed Manhattan Company (later renamed Chase Manhattan Bank) legally used, with the permission of Burr, surplus money to buy a private bank, thus breaking the stronghold the Federalists had on New York's capital. The new bank started lending to working-class citizens at a rate they could afford.

Angered and annoyed that he'd allowed himself to be used in this way, Hamilton vowed revenge when the time was right. A while later, when Burr and Thomas Jefferson were in a deadlock of seventy-three votes each for the presidency of the United States, Hamilton convinced his friends to vote for Jefferson. Burr lost the presidency and, according to the law at the time, became vice president instead. Now Burr was really mad.

After the election Burr learned of a private letter that was published in the *Albany Register.* The letter described Hamilton's forceful attack at a private dinner on Burr's personal character. (Up until this point, even though both men were angry at each other, they just considered all this the ugly side of politics, and they even dined together on occasion.) However, publicly insulting someone was another story. Burr felt he had to defend his honor and asked Hamilton to retract his statement. Hamilton refused to retract it or even admit he had expressed the "despicable opinion" at all.

Burr then felt obligated to save face, and in the style of an eighteenth-century gentleman, he challenged Hamilton to a duel. Hamilton felt compelled to accept. As he admitted privately to his friend Rufus King, he had been "extremely severe" in criticizing Burr and felt he must conform to the code of honor of the day. He accepted the duel but confided he would throw his first shot.

The date of the duel was set for July 11, 1804, at seven o'clock in the morning in New Jersey, just beneath the Palisades. One man, Moses King, wrote that the "dueling ground was a lonely grassy glade in the woods of Weehawken, high above the Hudson, allowing glimpses of New York through surrounding trees." (The area is just opposite today's Forty-second Street in Manhattan.)

Forty-nine-year-old Hamilton was opposed to dueling and was reluctant, even though he'd accepted, because just three years earlier he had lost his twenty-year-old son, Phillip, in a duel on the exact same grounds, using the exact same pistols. To Hamilton it was a lunatic way to solve a dispute, yet he could not withdraw without risking his honor. Forty-eight-year-old Burr, on the other hand, was blinded by public humiliation and charged ahead with bravado over bravery.

The day before the duel, Hamilton wrote out his will and got his affairs in order. On the fateful morning, he boarded a barge with his friend and second (a duel assistant), Nathaniel Pendleton, and Dr. David Hosack, a physician. He also brought the guns, two .56-caliber dueling pistols, as was his right since he was the one who had been challenged.

A cool vapor spread over the river as the oars made

gentle splashing sounds in the water on that summer morning. Dewdrops were still on the grass blades as Hamilton and his party reached their destination, slightly before the scheduled duel time. They climbed up the rocks to the appointed place.

Burr and his friends and seconds, William Van Ness and Matthew Davis, two leaders of the Society of St. Tammany, were already there. They had cleared some of the bushes away to make more space for the duel.

The two appointed seconds later collaborated and wrote, "When General Hamilton arrived, the parties exchanged salutations, then the seconds proceeded to make the arrangements. They measured the distance, ten full paces, and cast lots for the choice of position." Once that was done, "the pistols were loaded in each others presence, after which the parties took their positions."

The dueling rules were simple: The men would walk ten paces away from each other. The second would give the word and then shout "Present!" Once both replied "Present," they were free to fire at will. However, if one man fired before the other and missed, the other man had to say "One, two, three" and then fire or lose his turn. Both men indicated that they understood the rules.

The tension was immense. Only one man would walk away. In a matter of minutes, a soul would be snuffed from the planet because of some ill-spoken words. Who would it be?

Hamilton made a rather deliberate show of adjusting his spectacles and carefully sighting the barrel on his weapon before stepping into place. He did not want to be there, but it was too late to back out. The two men walked the ten paces.

On cue, the second yelled out, "Present!" Hamilton and Burr answered, then two shots were fired in quick succession. Hamilton's shot went high. Burr's shot was dead on. Burr's bullet lodged into Hamilton's spine, and immediately Hamilton fell. Burr moved towards Hamilton in regret, but before he could speak, he was quickly pulled away by one of his friends.

Burr left the field without saying a word.

Dr. Hosack rushed to Hamilton's side. Hamilton was sitting on the ground in Pendleton's arms. Just before he slipped into unconsciousness, he said, "This is a mortal wound, Doctor." The doctor immediately stripped Hamilton's clothes off, checked his pulse, and saw that his breathing had stopped. He could not feel a heartbeat. Dr. Hosack decided the only chance to save him was to get him on the barge and quickly get him home. Pendleton, the doctor, and the two bargemen carried Hamilton onto the boat. Dr. Hosack rubbed Hamilton's face, lips, and temples with spirits of hartshorn. He even applied it to his neck and chest, hoping it might have some effect.

Fifty yards from shore Hamilton breathed again and spoke, "My vision is indistinct." After a few more minutes, he said, "Take care of that pistol. It is undischarged and still cocked. It may go off and do harm. . . . Pendleton knows that I did not intend to fire at [Burr]." Then Hamilton closed his eyes and asked them to break the news gently to his wife.

Barely alive and in agony, Hamilton was carried to his home in Manhattan. The next day he died with his wife by his side.

As a result of this historical confrontation, Hamilton lost his life, and Burr fled to Philadelphia, a fugitive from the law in both New York and New Jersey. He was charged with two counts of murder, but not convicted since both men had agreed upon the duel. After his vice-presidential term ended, Burr never held office again. Later in life, Burr referred to "my friend Hamilton whom I shot" and often said, "If I had read Sterne more and Voltaire less, I should have known that the world was wide enough for Hamilton and me." A valuable lesson too late.

Now, the next time you look at a $10 bill and see the face of Alexander Hamilton, perhaps you will remember the lesson—and the real story.

The Incredible Jersey Jumper

· 1827 ·

The town of Paterson didn't quite know what to make of Sam Patch, a young cotton spinner who had just come down from Rhode Island about a year ago and worked in a local mill. Patch seemed to have had a run of bad luck. He had a prosperous mill all his own until his partner, a Scotsman by the name of Kennedy, ran off with all his money. Frustrated, Patch started to drink and began talking about how he used to jump the 100-foot-high Pawtucket Falls in Rhode Island. He claimed he'd done it often as a youngster. No one believed him. Then he tried to jump over the Great Falls of Paterson several times. Each time the local police caught him before he could jump and detained him overnight until he "sobered up."

But Patch was determined. He knew he was good at jumping, and he wanted to prove it. And then the opportunity came.

On September 29, 1827, the people of Paterson gathered to witness a new bridge being drawn across the rocky gorge above the Great Falls. The bridge had been the talk of the town for a while, since it was being built as part of a friendly competition between two local businessmen.

Tim Crane, a hotel owner, had noticed that a man by the name of Fyfield was making good money at his tavern across the gorge. Fyfield had about a hundred steps outside his tavern that went to the bottom of the falls. The Great Falls was a big attraction, and his place was always full. Crane wanted to give him a run for his money and build a place on the other side to capture some of the weekend trade. The best way to get access to the other side was to build a bridge. So he did.

The day came for the bridge to be swung into place. Sam Patch was in the crowd of onlookers. The police were nearby watching him to make sure he wouldn't try to jump.

On one side of the falls was the completed bridge. A bunch of ropes were attached to the bridge and tossed over to the other side, where they were then harnessed to a team of waiting horses that would pull the bridge slowly over the gorge and lodge it into place. The men cracked whips and tugged at the horses' harness with all their might. The ropes grew taut and began to strain from the weight of the bridge. The crowd held its breath in anticipation as the strength of the team of horses slowly lifted and pulled the bridge across, rolling it over wooden cylinders. While the bridge was moving across, with no land underneath to support it, it began to teeter. The structure swung precariously over the chasm. The crowd gasped.

The men on the other side of the falls shouted, grunted, and put their backs against the bridge, trying to balance it. The structure inched forward.

The bridge was halfway across when a loud cracking sound filled the air. The men pulling the bridge fell flat on their faces, and the horses were dragged backwards as they tried to hold the weight. A long wooden cylinder had fallen into the water, taking along with it one of the ropes that was needed to level the pulling. Without it, the bridge couldn't be pulled into place. This was not a good situation. The structure was now vertical—at any moment it could plunge into the Great Falls. As the crowd was pondering the fate of the bridge, out dashed Patch from behind a large dead oak tree at the top of the falls. He ran to the very edge of the gorge and shouted, "Old Tim Crane thinks he's done something great. But I can beat him!"

And with no more ceremony than that, twenty-year-old Sam Patch suddenly gave a tremendous vault and plunged 80 feet, feet first, toward the churning waters below. His arms hung by his sides. Down he went like a statue against the backdrop of the falls. For a moment the hanging bridge hid him from the crowd. At the last second they were able to see him spread his arms as if to break the fall. Then with a thud and a splash the water swallowed him up.

The onlookers forgot about the bridge and searched the shore for the crazed adventurer. Never before having seen such a spectacle, they didn't know if they had just witnessed a man's death or the greatest stunt ever performed.

A few moments later they had their answer. Like an agile serpent, first a head, then some shoulders emerged downstream from the falls. Patch looked around to orient himself to the shore. Before he crept up the jagged walls of the chasm, he grabbed the bridge's trailing guide rope and emerged out of the water, with not a bruise or the least sign of exhaustion. It was as if he had been out for a leisurely swim. The crowd broke into cheers and hugged one another. The lost bridge rope was gratefully taken from him. Hats were tossed in the air like confetti. The crowd hoisted their dripping hero onto their shoulders and started a paradelike procession up the bank. They placed him right in front of Tim Crane. Crane whispered something to him and Patch nodded. The crowd was silent, waiting for Patch's response. Then he spoke, "That's mighty generous of you, Mr. Crane. But I just wanted to show folks how some things can be done as well as others. And now I guess everyone knows there's no mistake in Sam Patch!"

The crowd cheered. Patch got his first taste of applause, and he liked it. He became the hero of the hour, and those two quotes became his trademarks. His career as the Jersey Jumper was born.

As for the bridge, the engineering marvel of its time, it was swung safely into place. The townspeople then gathered at Fyfield's tavern. They wanted to shake hands with and buy a drink for their own marvel, the man who had jumped the Great Falls.

Liking his newfound fame, and feeling he had discovered his purpose in life, Patch set out to make himself the best jumper the world had ever seen—not for money, but for the sheer pleasure of doing it. Although he did make $13 at one jump and $15 at another by passing around a hat, he never really made big money with his unusual skill. He was content living hand-to-mouth off the hospitality of others. In fact, the only person to make real money from Patch's jumps was a comedian by the name of Dan Marble who portrayed him years later in two plays, *Sam Patch* and *Sam Patch in France*. Still, Patch loved what he did, and he jumped the Great Falls several more times.

Patch made a show of every jump. As the *Journal of Commerce* put it, "Sam removed his coat, vest and shoes, and laid them carefully by, as if debating the question whether he should want them again." Then Patch would make a short speech, bow left and right, and finally "run forward and leap into the abyss."

His jumping style became well known for its technical mastery of precision and control. Like an arrow, he sped down to meet the foaming waters, striking without so much as a quiver, feet first, his hands coming down from over his head to below his hips, his feet drawn up, his knees straightening just before impact. He plunged into the water with hardly a splash. His trademark phrase, "Some things can be done as well as others," came to mean that it's not what you do in life that matters, but how well you do it.

Everyone had different opinions as to why Patch jumped. Some said it was for fame; others claimed it was to satisfy his ego; a couple even discounted his great feat altogether by claiming that "water in passing down the falls accumulates a large quantity of air and makes it almost impossible for a person to sink to any great depth" and that "the bottom of the falls becomes as soft as 'an ocean of feathers.'" Whatever his motive, multitudes came to see this brave daredevil jump and to listen to his simple philosophy on life.

The police gave up trying to stop or monitor Patch's jumps. He was told "to consult on his own safety and he leaps whenever it takes his fancy," said one official.

And fancy jumping he did. He liked the challenge so much that he decided to take his show on the road. He jumped everywhere and anywhere he could, from yardarms, factory walls, and ship masts. He toured the eastern United States, touted as the "Jersey Jumper" or the "Yankee Leaper." He was greeted as a celebrity wherever he went.

During one of his jumping tours, Patch got a fox and a small bear, and occasionally he was able to persuade the bear to jump with him—and even indulge in a drink or two to celebrate.

Then came the jump that immortalized him. Patch was invited to jump over Niagara Falls on October 6, 1829. A blast was planned to remove a rocky obstacle in the gorge over which Niagara plunged, and they wanted him to jump as part of the festivities. Though reluctant to share the billing, he agreed.

If he feared the falls he didn't show it. For the death-defying jump a special 125-foot ladder was rigged over the gorge below Goat Island opposite the Cave of the Winds. Bad weather and a delay in his arrival made the crowd small, but Patch, clad in white, with great deliberation put his hands close to his sides and jumped from the platform, a total of 80 feet down. A few minutes later he surfaced unharmed! The *Saturday Evening Post* reported, "Sam Patch has immortalized himself."

But why stop at immortality? Sam agreed to jump Niagara Falls again, on October 17 at precisely three o'clock in the afternoon, from 50 feet higher than he had a couple weeks before. This time a crowd of 10,000 watched him repeat his daring feat. Sam Patch was the first man ever to jump the falls and live, not once but twice. He not only leaped into the falls, but leaped into worldwide fame.

With the greatest waterfall in the United States conquered, Patch felt it was time to head to Europe and jump London Bridge. He wanted to show the European crowds that "some things can be done as well as others." He promised the folks in Rochester, New York, that he'd jump Genesee Falls before he left.

On November 6, 1829, "as all of Rochester congregated together," Patch jumped 100 feet from the Upper Falls accompanied by his pet bear. The town went wild; they said it was "an imposing spectacle." They weren't quite ready to lose their hero to Europe. They toasted him again and again and convinced him to do just one more jump. Patch reluctantly agreed. He didn't want to let his fans down. To make it even more spectacular, Patch announced it as his last jump, meaning his last jump in the United States.

He planned to do the final jump on none other than Friday, November 13—a leap into the abyss from a scaffold built 25 feet above Genesee Falls, making it a total jumping distance of 125 feet. This time he would jump alone without the bear. Maybe the bear was superstitious.

Some say Patch drank too much on that Friday. Some say the cold air and icy waters chilled him without warning. Some say it was bad luck due to Friday the 13th. Whatever it was, Patch, ironically, was right: It was his last jump.

He started out as poised as ever. Then, about a third of the way down, something went wrong. His body went limp. His legs separated, and he struck the water with a sickening smack.

No one wanted to believe he was dead. Some claimed he did it as a practical joke to gain more fame. In the next few weeks, there were Sam Patch sightings all over the country and reports of ghostly forms jumping Niagara Falls.

Contrary to popular belief, Patch's body was found two

days later, not four months later on St. Patrick's Day. The *Saturday Evening Post* reported that "it floated to shore a few rods below the spot where he came in contact with the water." His body was frozen in a block of ice.

An autopsy revealed he had suffered "the rupture of a blood-vessel, caused by the sudden chill of the atmosphere through which he passed to the water." Another report said that both of Patch's shoulders had been dislocated.

Death could not erase the memory of Sam Patch. He lived on via plays, books, and the memories of those who had witnessed the jumps of one of the greatest daredevils of all time. The *Saturday Evening Post* offered this poem:

> Hail to the hero, Samuel Patch!
>
> Who knows not any equal-
>
> In jumping, Sam can find no match
>
> Among ten million people.

The press, however, can be fickle, and after his death that same paper wrote that he was a "miserable vagabond" who catered to the "cruelty of the taste from strange spectacles."

Regardless of what was printed, to many Sam Patch was a symbol of bravery and fearlessness and an inspiration to follow your dreams no matter what anyone says. Sam lives on as a legend in New Jersey history.

The First Game
· 1846 ·

Most baseball fans believe the game as we know it was first played in 1839 in Elihu Phinney's cow pasture in Cooperstown, New York, conceived by a man named Abner Doubleday.

Unfortunately, that story is wrong.

The real beginning of baseball stems directly from an English children's game called rounders, the rules of which were published in *The Boy's Own Book* in London in 1829. The book was reprinted in America in 1835 under the title *The Boys and Girls Book of Sports*. The name "rounders" was changed to "base ball," and with this minor alteration, English rounders became American baseball. Thus the name and game of baseball was known to both English and American children long before Doubleday supposedly invented it.

The seeds of the Doubleday myth started in 1889 at a famous restaurant in New York City called Delmonico's. Three hundred people had gathered to celebrate a squad of professional ball players who had just returned from a world tour. Heading this team was the president of the Chicago Baseball Club, Albert G. Spalding, a major-league ace pitcher and the owner of a thriving sporting goods business. (Yes, Spalding balls!) At the banquet someone announced that "patriotism and research" had established that baseball was American in origin. Everyone cheered and considered the matter settled.

But it wasn't settled yet.

A few years later, in 1903, Henry Chadwick, the first great

baseball sportswriter, wrote an article pointing out the similar- ities of baseball to the English game of rounders. Wanting to discredit the rounders theory, Spalding put together a commis- sion of seven baseball experts, including two U.S. senators, to research the origin of baseball. After three years of testimony, a report was published on December 30, 1907, stating that baseball originated in the United States "according to the best evidence obtainable to date." That evidence was a hearsay let- ter from a Mr. Abner Graves, a supposed childhood friend of Abner Doubleday, who had a vague recollection of watching Doubleday play baseball some sixty-eight years prior.

Based solely on that letter, Abner Doubleday became a convenient figurehead and was dubbed the inventor of modern- day baseball. The reality? In 1839, the year baseball suppos- edly began, Abner Doubleday was a second-year West Point cadet whose family had moved out of Cooperstown in 1837. Had he been in Cooperstown at that time, he would have been AWOL from West Point.

Not once in his distinguished career as a writer, public speaker, or soldier who rose to the rank of general during the Civil War (and is credited with firing the first Union shot in defense of Fort Sumter) did Doubleday mention baseball. In fact, he wasn't even aware he was named its inventor! He died fourteen years before this honor was bestowed upon him. As baseball historian Harold Peterson said, "Abner Doubleday didn't invent baseball. Baseball invented Abner Doubleday." Thus the location of the Baseball Hall of Fame in Cooperstown, New York, is based on a myth, and, oddly enough, Doubleday was never inducted into the hall.

Perhaps that's because the truth is that Hoboken is the birthplace of baseball.

In 1846 Hoboken, a small, pleasant town of just one square mile, was a gorgeous paradise used mainly for recre- ational purposes. New York City was growing rapidly, and its sidewalks, streets, and buildings stretched out and consumed lush parks and grassy hills along the way, leaving little space for recreation. So many New Yorkers and New Jerseyans alike went to one particular area in Hoboken called Elysian Fields when they wanted green space.

Elysian Fields was a gorgeous five-acre paradise 1 mile from the Hudson River, where people could picnic, relax, or just get away from city life. It had trees, fresh spring water that flowed from the earth, and flowers of every color. In the midst of all this blooming beauty was a large grassy area, an ideal place to play a popular team sport of the day, cricket.

One sports enthusiast, however, thought it was an ideal place for something else. Alexander Joy Cartwright, the real and forgotten "Father of Baseball," thought it was a great place to play baseball.

Cartwright, a twenty-five-year-old, black-whiskered volunteer fireman, belonged to a firefighting organization called the New York Knickerbockers. When he wasn't fighting fires, he doubled as a bank teller at the Union Bank in New York City. He lived in an upscale home and was married to Eliza Gerrits Van Wie. And he loved to play a game then known as town ball (another American version of rounders that had been played for seventy-five years).

Since 1842 Cartwright and a group of about fifty select men both skilled in the game and of good standing in the community—seventeen merchants, twelve clerks, five brokers, four professional men, two insurance men, a bank teller, a "Segar Dealer," a hatter, a cooperage owner, a stationer, a U.S. marshal, and several other "gentlemen"—had gotten together to play town ball.

The game of town ball was very crude, with people being hit by the fast-moving ball in order to be struck out on their way to the bases. (It was more like dodgeball.) Those in the field would fight to catch the ball in a rather free-for-all manner.

After playing a few years by these rules, in 1845 Cartwright came up with an idea to form a baseball club. He made up twenty new rules (with the help of some suggestions from the president of the Knickerbockers, Daniel "Doc" Lucius Adams) for the club members to follow to make the game more civilized. He showed the rules to his town ball buddies, and they agreed to try the game with them. The rules were adopted on September 23, 1845, and Cartwright named his baseball club the New York Knickerbockers after his fire station.

Most of the new rules applied to the actual playing of the game, but the first rule, "Members must strictly observe the time agreed upon for exercise, and be punctual in their attendance," obviously was geared towards taking this game seriously. There were also established fines: 50 cents for refusing to obey the captain, 25 cents for disputing the decision of the umpire or even expressing an opinion on his verdict, and 6 cents for swearing.

According to a book called *The Jersey Game* by James M. DiClerico and Barry Pavelec, Cartwright took his newly formed team to New Jersey on the Hoboken Ferry. They walked the mile from the ferry to Elysian Fields in either late September or early October 1845 to play the first game by the new rules.

When they got to the field, they laid out a diamond and picked two captains to be in charge of the game. The captains, in turn, picked an umpire, and then they were ready to try out the newly revised game. They used several rules that are still part of baseball today: limiting a team to three outs per inning instead of the old rule of allowing the entire team to bat before switching; throwing the ball to bases to make outs rather than hitting the runner with the ball (a lot less painful); making the bases 90 feet apart; having only three outfielders instead of a free-for-all of an unlimited number of men; having "lineups" where each man had to bat in turn; having foul and safe lines made up; adding the position of shortstop; and having only nine men play on each side instead of a mob of men. Playing with these new guidelines changed baseball from a casual, reckless recreational game to one with rules and regulations.

Unfortunately, no one had a scorebook on hand, so the details of that first game are not known. It was reported several years later that there were forty-two runs scored in the game.

The gentlemen of the New York Knickerbockers liked the new rules so much they devoted every Monday and Thursday afternoon to "play days." But soon the team got tired of playing each other. Since they were the only ones playing by these rules, they claimed themselves world champs. Feeling rather confident, they challenged the "half-organized" Brooklyn Baseball Club to a match. The *New York Herald* carried a public notice of the game: "The New York Baseball Club will play a match of baseball against the Brooklyn Club tomorrow afternoon at 2 o'clock, at the Elysian Fields, Hoboken." Few spectators attended, and the details of this game weren't recorded.

However, one day that goes down in baseball history is June 19, 1846. It is known as "the day baseball was born." On that day, in Elysian Fields, the first real prearranged game of baseball between two separate organized clubs, the Knickerbockers and the New York Nines, was played using Cartwright's rules. A full account of that day and many other detailed facts are listed in the book *Baseball: The Early Years* by Harold Seymour. Here is the condensed story.

At two o'clock in the afternoon an uncounted number of spectators arrived in Hoboken. Male spectators stood on the sidelines, while the ladies sat under a canvas-covered pavilion or parasols to protect their complexions. The captains of each team met near home plate and chose an umpire to settle all disputes. The challenging club (the Nines) furnished the ball, and the winner would keep it as a trophy. The round bats were made of wood and not over $2\frac{1}{2}$ inches in diameter at the thickest part; they could be any length. No other equipment was used; there were no baseball gloves at the time.

All five stations—the canvas bases, home plate, and the pitcher's plate were painted or enameled in white. The champs, the Knickerbockers, were all decked out in their matching uniforms of blue pantaloons, white flannel shirts, and straw hats. The New York Nines didn't have a standard uniform. They weren't even exactly sure of all the Knickerbockers' rules. But they were game to play. They liked the fact that the pitcher had to throw a ball the batter liked, and it was said sometimes as many as fifty pitches went by before they'd swing. However, they were only allowed to miss three pitches of their choosing.

To anyone watching today, this odd way of pitching would be pretty amusing. The pitcher was not allowed to jerk or throw the ball to the batter. Instead, he had to toss it under-hand as near the plate as possible so that the batter would have the best opportunity to hit it. Talk about a gentlemen's sport— why not just hand him the ball?!

The New York Nines got the hang of it quickly, and the game went only four innings, because by that time the challengers had already scored twenty-one aces (runs), the necessary amount to win the game. But just for good measure, they scored another two, pummeling the Knickerbockers with Cartwright umpiring the game. The final score was 23 to 1. That day the New York Nines went home with their own ball.

The Knickerbockers dominated baseball, however, for a long time after that, and they sent out hundreds of copies of their rules to other clubs that asked. They played until the 1870s, when they built a clubhouse, and then faded into obscurity when other baseball teams started playing for money and turned it into a business.

As for Alexander Cartwright, he left the team in 1849 and traveled to California gold rush country with his rule book, baseball, and bat in hand. During his 156-day journey, he taught people in several different states—from saloon keepers to Indians, from miners to fortune seekers—the game as he had devised it. Every place his wagon visited got a dose of the Cartwright version of baseball. When he got to California, he felt it was too crowded, so he sailed with his brother to Hawaii, where he founded the Honolulu Fire Department and lived with his family. Cartwright died there in 1892, but not before teaching several Hawaiians the game.

When baseball celebrated its alleged one-hundred-year anniversary in Cooperstown in 1939, it was a big affair, with $100,000 in state money invested, parades, and star ballplayers on hand. The Baseball Hall of Fame was opened that year. The grandson of Alexander Cartwright, Bruce Cartwright, and the Hawaiian people got wind of this and sent tangible evidence of Cartwright's claim to the inventor's title and a plaque honoring him, demanding it be placed in the Hall of Fame. The centennial organizers researched the claim and soon it became apparent that it was legitimate. So they inducted Alexander Cartwright into the Hall of Fame along with the only known original copy of the rules. They then went ahead with the celebration anyway and continued to promote the Doubleday myth.

Today Elysian Fields is mostly covered by an abandoned coffee factory. The only bit of green left is a tiny park where parents still take their kids to play. Despite numerous efforts by politicians and lawyers and many hometown celebrations, Hoboken seems forgotten to the rest of the world as the place where baseball started. Only a plaque that says the following commemorates the spot: "On June 19, 1846 the first match game of baseball was played here on the Elysian Fields between The Knickerbockers and the New Yorks. It is generally conceded that until this time the game was not seriously regarded."

Baseball as we now know it started with Cartwright's vision to organize and lay down his twenty rules. Over time some rules were changed, others were added, and some were expanded to make baseball into the great American pastime we know today.

Santa Claus Is Born on a Desk in New Jersey

· 1862 ·

In a beautiful three-story home in Morristown, called Villa Fontana, a well-known artist by the name of Thomas Nast was having a bit of a problem. Nast had gotten a job at the leading magazine of the day, *Harper's Weekly,* during the bloodiest year of the Civil War. Thousands of Americans had lost their lives, and it was Nast's job to draw the battles, the soldier's life in camp, and other scenes of war. His drawings kept the Northern sympathies strong while the Confederate soldiers were winning battles. Nast was good at what he did, but today he was having illustrator's block because of a special request that had come from his editor, Fletcher Harper—a request that had been handed down straight from President Abraham Lincoln himself.

President Lincoln wanted Nast to draw "a special Christmas picture" for *Harper's* front page, a scene that would link Christmas to the ongoing war effort. Nast had no idea what to draw. He needed inspiration, and quick, since the deadline was approaching.

Nast's sister Bertha, a New York City schoolteacher, happened to be visiting him at his home that day. He talked to

Bertha about the drawing he had to make, and they both started reminiscing about their childhood in Germany. They talked about the differences between the German Pelznickel and the American Santa Claus, who up to this point had been drawn as a short, stumpy man with a thin, hawklike face with sharp features. His eyes were sinister, and in some cases when he had a beard, it was scrawny. His clothing ranged from an overcoat and pants to an Arabian prince outfit complete with puffy sleeves.

Bertha mentioned that her students got into the Christmas spirit by reading *A Visit from Saint Nicholas* (better known as "'Twas the Night before Christmas"). They talked some more, and by the time Bertha left, Nast was inspired. He worked through the night giving Santa Claus a makeover, trying to create a symbol for Christmas and comfort for the soldiers.

The next morning the weary-eyed Nast delivered his finished drawings to *Harper's*. On January 3, 1863, the Christmas edition of the magazine hit the stands. On the cover was a drawing entitled "Santa in Camp." It showed a fat jolly man with a modern-length white beard and big red cheeks. Nast's Santa also had the now-famous twinkle in his eye. He was dressed in a patriotic furry Stars and Stripes outfit with a big black belt around his middle. Santa was shown visiting Union soldiers in camp, distributing Christmas gifts from his sleigh. The picture was filled with activity. One soldier was opening his present to find a fully loaded stocking. A soldier behind him was happy with his meerschaum pipe gift. In the foreground a jack-in-the-box was popping out, surprising two drummer boys. In the background some soldiers were playing football, while others were chasing around a greased pig. Other soldiers were preparing Christmas dinner. Everyone was happy. To top it all off, soldiers at the fort at the top of the picture were giving Santa an artillery salute.

Inside the magazine an article explained all the things on the cover. There were also several more Christmas scenes in that same issue, all of which countered the image people had of lonely soldiers in the cold during the holiday season. An article titled "Children" read, "You mustn't think Santa Claus comes to you alone." The article explained how Santa brought a stack of *Harper's Weekly* magazines to the soldiers so that "they as well as you little folks, may have a peep at the Christmas number."

Nast's Christmas images were a huge success. Not only did he give us our modern-day Santa through those drawings, but he also captured the joy and excitement of the season perfectly. The release of his images was called "one of the most demoralizing moments for the Confederate army." Ulysses S. Grant even said that Nast "did as much as any man to preserve the Union and bring the war to an end."

And so began a tradition. Every year until his departure from *Harper's* in 1886, Nast drew images of Santa Claus, constantly refining him. The year following the first issue, Santa looked even kinder and was given a red suit and a home at the North Pole. Nast later drew Santa poring over a list of naughty and nice children. He added Santa's workshop and images of him being whisked away by his reindeer in his sleigh. He even gave him a pipe. The final touch came when Nast was asked to draw a series of color pictures of Santa for a book about Santa Claus. That's when he added the trimmed white fur to his red outfit.

By the time Nast left *Harper's* he was famous not only for his pictures of Santa, but also for his political cartoon symbols of the Republican elephant and the Democratic donkey. He donated his talents to local theater productions and to benefits for local hospitals.

Unfortunately, Nast did not come to a jolly ending himself. Disgusted by political corruption (his cartoons played a large part in the downfall of the corrupt Boss Tweed administration), he left *Harper's*, went into a financial crisis, and was forced to give up his home—the home where the Santa Claus that we know and love was created. Down on his luck, he moved to

Guayaquil, Ecuador, having accepted a consular post. But after just six months there, on December 7, 1902, he died of yellow fever at the age of sixty-two.

But if Nast is looking down from the heavens, he can at least be happy to know that his Santa Claus made it to the top. According to a December 2002 *Forbes* magazine poll, Santa is considered the richest person in the "Forbes Fictional Fifteen" list, beating out Daddy Warbucks, Scrooge McDuck, and Richie Rich and praised for "having devoted a lifetime of Christmases trying to fruitlessly give away his fortune to little children."

Grim Lottery
of Death
· 1864 ·

It was a fine Monday in March of 1864. The streets of Cape May were lined with banners and people anxiously waiting to give a hero's welcome to Captain Henry Washington Sawyer of the First New Jersey Cavalry. As he came into sight, he was greeted by his loving and devoted wife and children. Despite his weak physical state resulting from being confined and "entirely without meat for the last forty days of his imprisonment," he was in good spirits and was determined to stay in active service until August of 1865. But for now, he was moved as the town welcomed his return and bestowed upon him a medal of honor from the Pennsylvania legislature for being a man of courage, strength, and pride.

This was a true day for celebration because, in fact, the days leading up to it, and the events surrounding it, were shrouded in tense decision and misery.

At age nineteen, Henry Washington Seager decided to leave the family farm in Pennsylvania, study carpentry, and head out to Cape May, a town in the midst of a construction boom. His father was incensed and threatened to disown Henry, and Henry never saw him again. Little did either of them know, Henry's decision to leave would years later have a great impact on the fate of New Jersey and the Civil War.

Upon moving to Cape May, Henry changed his German

last name from Saeger to Sawyer, married a local girl with *Mayflower* ties, Harriet Ware Eldredge, had two children, and did some odd-and-end construction jobs.

Then, on April 15, 1861, life changed for Henry. President Abraham Lincoln issued a proclamation asking for volunteers to serve in the War between the States. Henry was the first man in the entire county to volunteer. In fact, he enlisted so early there wasn't even a regiment for him to join. So the governor of New Jersey sent Henry to Washington, D.C., with secret dispatches for the Union's secretary of war. Henry performed his duties so well that he was given several merits. At that time the enlistment period was only ninety days. By the time his ninety days were up, Henry Washington Sawyer was already second sergeant. He enlisted again, and by February of 1862 he was a lieutenant, Company D, First New Jersey Cavalry. By October of that year he was a captain.

In June 1863, Sawyer was severely wounded by two bullets at the Battle of Brandy's Station. a bloody combat that pitted twenty thousand Union and Confederate soldiers against one another. One bullet pierced his thigh and another tore through his right cheek and exited out of the back of his neck on the left side of his spine. Sawyer was left for dead. When he regained consciousness on the battlefield, he noticed a fallen friend and tried to work his way over to him. Rebel soldiers spotted him moving, took him prisoner, and brought him to Libby Prison in Richmond, Virginia, where he was expected to die. But he didn't—a worse fate awaited him.

Libby Prison, named after Captain Luther Libby, who leased the building at the outbreak of the Civil War and was forced to turn it over within forty-eight hours to serve as a hospital and prison, had a horrible reputation. The prisoners were held in a cellar vault that was only 6 feet wide and had no light or air circulation except for a 6-inch-square hole cut into the door. Rats infested the building, and prisoners were responsible for cooking their own food, so they often fought amongst themselves for cooking pots. Time went by slowly, and cards were used until the spots wore off.

As Sawyer grew stronger, he assumed he would soon be exchanged for a Confederate prisoner of war, which was a common practice. Unfortunately for him, the timing couldn't have been worse. Apparently, General Ambrose Burnside had executed two Confederate captains two weeks earlier in Kentucky, and the Confederacy was screaming for revenge. An eye for an eye—they wanted two Northern captains dead.

On July 4 Confederate General John H. Winder, Provost-Marshal General, head of all the Confederate prisons in 1863, issued a special order stating that two of the seventy-five Union captains held in Libby Prison were to be selected for execution. The captains were brought to a large room, told of the order, and asked how they wished their fate to be chosen.

Captain Sawyer yelled out, "Let Chaplain Brown do the job!" Despite the fact that it was against war rules, three chaplains had been imprisoned with the soldiers. The men agreed with Sawyer's choice. Each man put his name on a piece of paper and folded it. The papers were then placed in a box. Showing visible emotion, Chaplain Brown, of the Sixth Maryland Regiment, accepted the task. A *Richmond Dispatch* reporter, whose name is unknown, witnessed the event. He wrote:

> Amid a silence almost deathlike, the drawing commenced. The first name taken out of the box was that of Captain Henry Washington Sawyer, of the First New Jersey cavalry, and the second that of Captain John Flinn, of the Fifty-First Indiana. When the names were read out, Sawyer heard it with no apparent emotion, remarking that some one had to be drawn, and he could stand it as well as any one else. Flinn was very white and depressed. With the drawing over, the prisoners were returned to their quarters

and the condemned proceeding under guard to the headquarters of General Winder, Provost-Marshal General. Here they were warned not to delude themselves with any hope of escape, as retaliation must be and would be inflicted, it being added that the execution would positively take place on the 14th, eight days hence.

Flinn considered himself a beaten man. But Sawyer felt as long as he was alive, there was hope. He asked permission to write a letter to his wife back in New Jersey. It was granted on the condition that the prison authorities would read the letter before sending it.

Sawyer carefully composed the letter, hoping that his wife would read between the lines and bring it to Union authorities so that he might still be rescued. Below is the letter in its entirety:

Provost-General's Office.
Richmond, Va.
July 6, 1863

My Dear Wife: — I am under the necessity of informing you that my prospects look dark.

This morning all the captains now prisoners at the Libby Military Prison drew lots for two to be executed. It fell to my lot. Myself and Captain Flinn, of the Fifty-First Indiana Infantry, will be executed for two captains executed by Burnside.

The Provost-General J. H. Winder, assures me that the Secretary of War of the Southern Confederacy will permit yourself and my dear children to visit me before I am executed. You will be permitted to bring an attendant, Captain Whilldin, or Uncle W. W. Ware, or Dan, had better come with you. My situation is hard to be borne, and I cannot think of dying without seeing you and the children.

You will be allowed to return without molestation to your home. I am resigned to whatever is in store for me, with the consolation that I die without having committed any crime, but it fell to my lot. You will proceed to Washington. My government will give you transportation for Fortress Monroe, and you will get here by a flag of truce, and return the same way. Bring with you a shirt for me.

It will be necessary for you to preserve this letter to bring evidence to Washington of my condition. My pay is due me from the first of March, which you are entitled to. Captain B—owes me fifty dollars, money lent to him when he went on a furlough. You will write to him at once, and he will send it to you.

Farewell! Farewell!! And I hope it is all for the best. I remain yours until death.

H. W. Sawyer
Captain
First New Jersey Cavalry

Immediately after writing the letter, Sawyer and Flinn were placed in the dungeon with a round-the-clock guard whose purpose was to call out their names every half hour to make sure they were still alive and did not commit suicide. The men, already stressed, had little chance for sleep. On top of that, rats scurried around the cell. Conditions were grim.

To make matters even worse, their cell was situated right next to a room used to store dead bodies. The guards would wait until the room was filled to capacity before "taking out the bodies" like one does with the trash. This was in the heat of the Southern summer; the stench was unbearable.

Mrs. Sawyer received the letter on July 13, only three days before the scheduled execution. She immediately took action and went with Captain Whilldin to Washington by stagecoach. By 10:00 P.M. the next night she was in front of President Lincoln, who promised to help. Lincoln sent for Secretary of War Edwin Stanton.

Stanton ordered that two officers "not below the rank of captain" be held as counterhostages. One of those officers was General "Rooney" Lee (son of the famed General Robert E. Lee), who had been injured on the same day, June 9, in the same battle as Sawyer, and had been taken prisoner by the Union. A letter was sent to the South proclaiming that if Sawyer, Flinn, or any other captain or Northern prisoner "not guilty of crimes punishable with death by the laws of war" were executed, then Rooney Lee and a General Winder, son of rebel Provost-Marshal General J. H. Winder, would die in retaliation.

The county of Cape May, which had been neutral and vulnerable until this point since it was a border region, joined the Union cause as a result of Sawyer's tragic letter. (Many historians believe this county was also a part of Harriet Tubman's Underground Railroad system.)

Each side waited, delaying the fate of the four men scheduled for execution. Neither Sawyer nor Flinn knew what Sawyer's letter had led to, so they waited each passing hour thinking they were getting closer to the hour of execution.

The message had the desired effect: July 16 came and went without either captain being executed. But for another eight months, Sawyer and Flinn languished in the cell, not knowing what would happen. They only had the Richmond newspapers to go by, and those stated that "the execution must and would take place." Sawyer, as the *Richmond Dispatch* reported, held up remarkably, with "unfaltering courage, steady and calm." He was quoted as saying, "If we may do so without impropriety, I am determined that New Jersey should have no cause to be ashamed of my conduct." Flinn, on the other hand, was doing very poorly.

On March 23, 1864, an exchange of prisoners took place—Lee for Sawyer and Winder for Flinn. The prisoners shook hands, grateful that their lives were spared in the lottery of death.

Sawyer returned to Cape May and received his hero's welcome. He remained in active service, was wounded twice again, and returned home permanently as a lieutenant colonel. "The Colonel," as he was known, became a councilman and official greeter and proprietor of the Ocean House, one of Cape May's largest hotels. In 1875 he built Sawyer's Boarding House at 301 Howard Street, later changing the name of the establishment to Chalfonte Hotel. The landmark hotel still stands and now is one of the foremost resorts in Cape May.

True to his upright reputation, while Sawyer was alive the Chalfonte Hotel catered to Southern clientele. A man who obviously did not hold a grudge, Sawyer said, "After the war, where once blood flowed, flowers now grow. We are one people again and the greatest country of the world. All is forgiven."

Two Noons over Jersey

· 1883 ·

Imagine that your friend from Washington, D.C., calls you to invite you to an important impromptu dinner date with some big executives. You can't be late, he tells you. You need to take the noon train out of Trenton or you will miss the meeting. You look at your watch. No problem, you can make it to the station by noon. You rush to get ready, and you get to the Trenton train station with two minutes to spare. But the train has already left. How can that be? It's exactly 11:58 A.M. The problem is that in Washington, D.C., it's noon. In Trenton it's already 12:10 P.M. You've missed the train, the meeting, and a big opportunity. That's the way it was before a New Jersey man by the name of William F. Allen set out to change the way we tell time.

Allen brought standard time to the United States on November 18, 1883, just seven months after he announced he would engineer a way to switch time so everything could run smoothly. A monumental plan to announce, even more so to execute.

For thousands of years, people measured time based on the position of the sun. When the sun was highest in the sky, no matter where you were, it was considered noon. This was and is called apparent solar time. Sundials were used into the Middle Ages, and then clocks began to appear. But even then, cities would set their town clocks by measuring the position of the sun, so every city ran on a slightly different time. This was fine if no one ever left his or her hometown, but when passenger travel by railroad was made available, schedules became hectic. With apparent solar time there were seventy different local time zones. For each 13 miles traveled westward, a person would have to set his watch back by a minute. Railroads used their home station time, thus three or four trains could converge into one station because each had used its own time.

Punctuality was a matter of guesswork, luck, or faith. For the railways it was a matter of chaos.

Enter William F. Allen, the son of a Bordentown railroad man and a railroad man himself from the tender age of sixteen. To him, time meant everything. By the time he was twenty-six, Allen was so fascinated by trains and their schedules that he became the editor of the *Official Guide of the Railway and Steam Navigation Lines*. This job was a big undertaking since the timetables were so confusing. Allen could not eradicate the sun, but he could make it work to his benefit. In 1875 Allen became the secretary of the General Time Convention, which has since become the American Railway Association. Allen was determined to make time a servant, not a master that had to be listened to every 13 miles.

Basing his plan on an idea that a Professor Dowd of Saratoga, New York, had conceived (the first American who had tried to make time behave and had devised a plan back in 1869, which was never accepted), Allen divided the country into four equal time zones along the 75th, 90th, 105th, and 120th meridians. He was determined to find a way to make this work in practice, not just in theory.

While Allen worked out the details of his plan, he faithfully moved his watch ahead a minute each morning as he commuted to New York City and then back a minute each night as he returned home to South Orange. Each time he changed his watch, he was more determined to have his plan come into action. Until then, like every other commuter, he had to check the "Comparative Time-Table" schedule to make sure he would catch his train. This schedule was more like a mathematical scorecard than a train schedule, listing the comparative times in 102 major cities.

For example, if the "Comparative Time-Table" schedule showed that it was noon in Washington, D.C., then it was 12:14 in Albany, 11:41 in Augusta, Georgia, 12:02 in Baltimore, and 11:06 in New Orleans. A note at the top of the schedule summed up the frustration of railroad employees:

> There is no "Standard Railroad Time" in the United States or Canada; but each railroad company adopts independently the time of its own locality, or at that place which its principal office is situated. The inconvenience of such a system, if system it can be called, must be apparent to all, but is most annoying to persons strangers to the fact. From this cause many miscalculations and misconnections have arisen, which not infrequently have been of serious consequence to individuals, and have, as a matter of course, brought into disrepute all RailRoad-Guides, which of necessity give the local times. In order to relieve, in some degree, this anomaly in American railroading, we present the following table of local time, compared with that of Washington, D.C.

The pamphlet then listed the 102 major cities and their local times alphabetically. It went on to say, "By an easy calculation the difference in time between the several places above named may be ascertained . . . and remember that places West are 'slower' in time than those East and visa versa."

No one could simply *ride* the train, they had to do the Pythagorean theorem just to get somewhere on time!

Finally fed up with the inconsistencies, in April 1883 the

General Time Convention committee in charge of the railroads announced that effective November 18, 1883, Mr. William F. Allen would have a plan perfected that would make time conform to man. (*NOTE:* Some history books credit Canadian civil engineer Sandford Fleming as instigating the initial efforts to adopt a time change and being a strong advocate of the adoption of standard time.)

Allen figured out that there should be an hour's difference in each of his four time zones. Time "slowed" in a westward pattern. So, for example, in the 75th meridian zone from Maine to a little west of Pittsburgh, it would be noon everywhere within that zone as soon as the sun moved across that longitude. So when it was noon in the 75th meridian zone from Maine to a little west of Pittsburgh, it was 11:00 A.M. in the next time zone west, 10:00 A.M. in one after that, and so on.

Most people liked the idea since it seemed to be a solution to the railroad-scheduling problem. Of course, as with any new plan, there were also critics. A few newspaper reporters claimed the change was "contrary to nature," some church folk felt it was "tampering with God's law," and the attorney general of the United States warned the federal agencies that they were *not* to accept the "Allen Plan" without an act of Congress.

Allen ignored all the naysayers. According to the only known documented source on the time change, a pamphlet issued by the Association of American Railroads entitled "The Day of Two Noons" by Carlton Corliss, the adjustment to the new time zones called for careful planning and preparation. Orders were issued by Allen from New Jersey "onto every division, instructing every officer and every employee as to what should be done. Train crews on line were instructed as to what change to make." With all the careful planning in place, on Sunday, November 18, 1883, as the sun passed over the 75th, then 90th, then 105th, and finally 120th longitudes, every railroad clock east of the lines was stopped until the second when the sun had crossed the newly set governing lines. Clocks west of that point had to be adjusted at the exact same time. It took massive coordination and effort on the part of all the railroads in all the states across the country. It was the ultimate act of precision timing, engineered to the split second, and it was pulled off without a hitch and without federal legislation of any sort! Allen was one of the few men in the world who could actually say he made time stand still.

The day became known in history as the "Day of Two Noons" since every town east of the controlling lines first had it's noon according to the sun, then minutes later had the newly established standard time noon. In some places, such as Georgia, the gap was forty-four minutes apart! The railroads had made the country conform.

The United States Congress was more stubborn. They didn't agree upon standard time until thirty-five years later, on March 19, 1918, during the First World War, when they instituted both standard and daylight saving time—a double whammy.

Ironically, the attorney general who so stubbornly refused to accept the "Allens Plan" refused to change his watch on the Day of Two Noons. As he went to catch a train that night, the results hit home. He arrived at the railroad station on time according to the old "sun time," but the train had pulled away from the station eight minutes and twenty seconds earlier, according to new standard time.

To this day people still oppose standard time as well as daylight saving time. One nonconformist wrote, "I don't really care how time is reckoned so long as there is some agreement about it, but I object to being told that I am saving daylight when my reason tells me that I am doing nothing of the kind. . . . As an admirer of moonlight I resent the bossy insistence of those who want to reduce my time for enjoying it."

Time zones have changed since Allen's ingenious plan was put into action. In fact, they are still changing. The Department of Transportation conducts rule making sessions to consider requests for changes. Generally, time zone boundaries shift westward. By law, the principle standard for deciding on a time zone change is for "the convenience of commerce." Good thing the commerce determining the changes isn't working the night shift, or we'd all be standing in the dark.

The Legendary Blizzard

· 1888 ·

On Saturday, March 10, 1888, the weather in New Jersey, and, in fact, along the entire eastern coast, was so pleasant that families had outdoor picnics. The temperature was in the fifties, and the mildest winter season in seventeen years was drawing to a close.

The main weather station at the time was the U.S. Army Signal Corps in Washington, D.C. That agency was in charge of making weather "indications," as predictions were called back then.

Three times a day, 154 local weather stations around the country telegraphed data about their surrounding regions to the D.C. office. The information included barometric pressure, humidity, temperature, wind velocity and direction, cloudiness, and precipitation. Then the D.C. office took all this information, marked it on maps, and analyzed it. The Signal Corps was proud of its efficiency and claimed an 82 percent accuracy rate.

They were even more proud of the man who headed the Signal Corps, Adolphus W. Greely, a famous polar explorer. If anyone was going to know about weather, he was the man.

On March 10 there were reports of two storms, one sweeping across Minnesota, Wisconsin, and Michigan, which would probably dump some snow along the way, and one in the South, which was moving over the warm waters of the Gulf of Mexico and dragging along moisture-laden air.

After carefully analyzing the data, Greely decided that neither storm would pose a real problem for anyone. The northern storm was losing its strength, and the southern one was on its way out to sea. The Signal Corps's report for the next couple days read, "Fresh to brisk winds, with rain, will prevail, followed on Monday by colder brisk westerly winds and fair weather throughout the Atlantic states."

The New York City Weather Station received this information. This station was also monitored by a man who had survived subzero temperatures on an Arctic expedition, Sergeant Francis Long. Long looked at the information, combined it with his own last-minute readings, and sent out a message to New Jersey and other eastern states, "Fresh to brisk southerly winds, slightly warmer, fair weather, followed by rain." With that done, Long and the rest of the New York staff closed the station at midnight and went home to observe the Sabbath. For the next seventeen hours, no one across the nation would be monitoring the changing weather patterns.

While innocent people slept, an unbridled, unmonitored monster was gathering strength. The two storm systems joined into one massive force, the northern storm armed with snow and bitter cold and the southern storm with a battery of moist gale winds. Together they were getting ready to bring an immense wrath upon the eastern coast. The legendary blizzard of 1888 was about to begin.

Menace could be felt in the air. On Sunday morning as the dark, ominous clouds hung low, a minister in a small New Jersey village looked up. "It was as if the unholy one himself was riding in on those clouds," he reported. He hurried indoors and prayed for mercy, but the sounds of the storms must have drowned out his prayers. For the next three days, a storm of epic proportion raged so powerfully that meteorologists considered it a 500-year event.

By late Sunday morning the majority of working-class and

commercial business people had rushed home after church to settle in for a cozy day indoors. Almost all the restaurants, theaters, shops, and concert halls were closed to observe the strict Sabbath laws, so it was either stay home or go visiting. Some chose the latter option, for no matter how threatening the weather looks, there are those who will chance fate. Adults visited while kids played in the streets. A few men found their way to beer halls illegally open on the Sabbath.

Those with no option were the workers who had a job to do despite the weather, those individuals who kept the city running smoothly. They were the train engineers and conductors, operators of horse-drawn carriages, doctors, ministers, priests, rabbis, telegraph operators, bridge operators, policemen, and firefighters. And, of course, there were the farmers who made up over half of the U.S. population at the time and whose animals didn't know what the Sabbath meant.

Meanwhile, the ocean was choppy and restless. Steamships, schooners, and tugboats hurried into the safety of the bays. There was something these tough, rugged seamen knew, for they were not easy to intimidate.

However, despite the plunging barometer that promised an intense storm, nine pilot boats bobbed as they waited off the coast of Sandy Hook for the big freight-carrying vessels to come in. According to the shipping news, at least six big ocean liners were due in port any moment, and the first pilot boat to race out and greet her got to guide her in.

By three o'clock in the afternoon, rain had begun to fall, and the wind picked up. The few people on the streets went inside to escape the bitter weather. The homeless sought shelter in alleyways and hallways.

By five o'clock, the New York City Weather Station had had the staff report in to collect fresh data. There was only one problem: Telegraph contact with the Washington, D.C., office was cut off.

The pilot boat captains at Sandy Hook were the first to

taste the bitter storm. The winds suddenly shifted, wind velocity increased, the temperature dropped, and they were instantly surrounded by a blinding snowstorm. The ships in the harbors up and down the New York and New Jersey coast bounced like toys in a bathtub. Masts broke, and ships ripped away from piers and were smashed against each other. Boats were tossed onto the beach, and damaged vessels began to sink. Those who managed to get off their boats and swim to shore were further ravaged by whirling beach sand. Professional lifesavers had their hands full rescuing survivors from seventeen schooners and freighters that had already gone aground. The waves were already 15 feet high, and this was just the beginning.

By six o'clock, a mix of frigid air and warm water had caused the storm's moisture to condense into icy rain and snow. At the same time hurricane-force winds developed. Within an hour temperatures plummeted twenty degrees and continued to drop over the next several hours. (In Tom's River the temperature dropped from forty-four to fourteen degrees in forty-eight hours!)

The *New Jersey Courier* described what happened next: "The first blast of the storm, after the shift of the wind, was terrific, and most of our residents were aroused by the rocking of their houses upon their foundations. With the wind came snow, flying, swirling, drifting before the blast and by seven o'clock fully one foot of snow had fallen, which, however, was piled upon drifts some of which attained the height of five or six feet." People who were out visiting decided to head home before the storm got any worse, but they encountered several obstacles.

A thick ice had built up on the streets, making it difficult to walk. Vicious wind-driven sleet changed into tiny sharp ice particles that slashed at people's faces, forcing them to close their eyes and have to make their way blindly through the streets. Since most weren't dressed for this weather, exposed areas of their bodies, like their ears and hands, were numbed. A trip that might normally take one hour now took two.

By Monday, March 12, the blizzard was in full force, claiming its turf from Delaware to Maine. Today the U.S. Weather Service defines a blizzard as a storm with winds of more than 35 miles per hour and snow that limits visibility to 500 feet or less. A severe blizzard has winds exceeding 45 mph, visibility of less than 0.75 mile, and temperatures of ten degrees or lower. The Great White Hurricane, as the 1888 storm was later called, had temperatures below zero with winds clocked at 100 miles per hour!

That Monday morning, despite the weather, thousands tried to make it to work for fear of losing their jobs. Few laws were in place protecting workers' rights. Workers were routinely fired for being late or absent. Job security was fragile in 1888—those who had jobs were lucky, and they weren't about to let a little snow stand in their way of feeding their families.

It was also a matter of habit and duty, and people simply didn't understand the dangers that the storm imposed. So sheer determination made people go to work and hundreds of children trudge to school only to find the schoolhouses closed. Stories of heroism abounded. One schoolmaster tied ropes to all the children who showed up and then dropped them at their homes one by one so none were lost. A policeman named Longe carried three schoolteachers from the Number 12 School in Bergen Heights home on his back.

Another determined soul was milkman William Brubacker, who awoke at half past one in the morning, hitched up his horse and wagon, went to the Hudson River, crossed on the ferry to his Jersey City route, and attempted to deliver the bottled milk to customers. A couple of hours later, his ears were painfully frozen and exhaustion was setting in. He stopped at a saloon and gulped down a glass of whiskey, which in those days was considered the best medicine for fighting off colds and frostbite. (It was even given to women and children as a surefire remedy.) Brubacker decided to turn his horse toward home, saying the horse "had more sense than I" since it had been trying to head back to the stable since they'd started out.

Meanwhile, at the Singer Sewing Machine factory in Elizabeth, 1,800 out of the 3,200 workers arrived on time. Three of those workers, seventeen-year-old James Marshall and his two friends, Alexander Bennett and Charles Lee, almost didn't make it. They had rowed their boat to work half a mile across the choppy waters of Newark Bay, as they had done every morning. About a 150 feet from shore, with the waves pounding and their faces frozen from the icy waters, they tried to turn around. Suddenly the wind shifted and pushed them to shore.

But not everyone was so lucky. By noon the Singer factory workers were told to go home. The women decided they'd never make it and stayed in the building. The men, figuring there was enough testosterone in groups of twenty to beat a mere snowstorm, ventured home. After all, it was half a mile to the train station. Many didn't make it. One witness described what happened: "Men's eyelids were frozen and people were groping along blindly. As I reached the train station, six men had been terribly frozen on the way. The hands of some of them, the ears of others and even portions of their bodies were frozen. I have no doubt that [many men] were buried in the drifts."

James Marshall and his buddies were among those trying to make it home. They got in their rowboat and attempted to row back to Staten Island. The boat bottomed out, and they landed several miles from their target location. They found a nearby farm and tried to keep themselves warm in the haystack. They were wet, cold, hungry, tired, and barely conscious. Marshall tried to convince his friends to keep moving. They stopped moving and eventually died. After the storm was over, the owner of the farm found Marshall mumbling incoherently. His hands and feet had to be amputated.

As the storm continued swirling, everything else was at a

standstill. Transportation of every kind was paralyzed. Horses were abandoned with their carriages, and later their corpses were found in snowdrifts. Those carriage owners who did try to work, and make an enormous profit by charging people an outrageous $100 a ride, eventually had to stop simply because they couldn't get through the streets.

Every hotel was filled to capacity with stranded passengers. Customers reported seeing frozen birds dropping dead to the ground from their windows. (Approximately 500 birds died in the storm.) Those people who couldn't afford hotels or couldn't make it to one, and were too far from home or work, were graciously given refuge in private homes.

On farmlands, cows froze in pastures. Sheep and goats blindly drifted into nearby ponds and drowned. One farmer, on his way to feed his animals, lost his way in the snow and relentless wind. He died 30 feet from his front door.

On top of dealing with nature's harshness, no food or supplies of any kind could be brought into the cities. Since Monday was the big delivery day for meats, fish, and all kinds of food, grocery stores quickly ran out, and there was no way to get more. As the *Newark Evening News* reported, "Unless the railroads are cleaned and trains are running by Friday many Newarkers will go hungry for nearly every kind of food, except that made with flour." People feared a famine as they watched their babies cry for milk and their children huddle together to try to keep warm.

There were more problems to deal with. People had to watch out for downed electric lines, and there were no litter laws in place at the time. Newspapers, household garbage, broken glass, 500,000 pounds of manure, and 60,000 gallons of horse urine were hardened into chunks that were picked up with the winds and thrown in people's faces!

On Monday night a Vermont newspaper, the *Bellows Falls Times,* summed up the situation best: "No paths, no streets, no sidewalks, no light, no roads, no guests, no calls, no teams, no hacks, no trains, no moon, no meat, no milk, no paper, no mails, no news, nothing—but snow."

On Tuesday morning, March 13, the storm was as vicious as ever. Those who had stayed home on Monday felt they had to go to work on Tuesday. City officials tried to figure out a way to clear railroad paths to get people safely to their destinations so they wouldn't freeze to death on the trains. Streets had to be cleared so emergency vehicles could get through. This was at a time when city governments did not see snow removal as a part of their responsibility. They usually would just let the snow melt, or at least wait until the storm had stopped. But in this case they couldn't wait. All the eastern cities were paralyzed. They had to do something—thousands of lives were at stake.

In New York and New Jersey, thousands of Italian immigrants were hired to shovel the streets and dig out the railroads. In all, 17,000 workers hand-removed twenty-four-million cubic yards of snow just to get traffic moving.

And where was all that snow moved to? It was piled in front of businesses, homes, hotels, and apartment buildings. Piles of snow were so high that one lady said, "It was most strange to see sleighs at the level of some second floor windows."

Industrious boys used shovels, brooms, and ice choppers, charging $5.00 to $25.00 an hour to store owners to remove the snow. Other boys brought ladders and stretched them down to the frozen East River so people could climb down and walk across to jobs on the other side. Unfortunately, as hundreds of people were sliding across on the ice, three powerful tugboats came along, breaking a path in the water to make a route for the other boats. People ended up floating on ice chunks in the middle of the river! Fortunately, most made it to shore.

In Camden there were different water problems. The strong blizzard winds combined with the low tides literally blew out all the water in the Delaware River. The water level dropped so low that Camden's water pumps would not work, causing a severe water shortage.

Finally, on Wednesday, March 14, the blizzard was officially over.

Many businesses tried to open using humor as a way to deal with the financial loss and to lift spirits. One Newark businessman put a sign outside his store: 500 GIRLS WANTED . . . TO EAT SNOW. Another Jersey businessman wrote 1,000 POUNDS OF FREE SNOW WITH EVERY $1 PURCHASE.

A frustrated shopkeeper in New York put a sign outside his business reading IMPORTANT! EXPENSIVE DIAMOND RING LOST UNDER THIS SNOW DRIFT! FINDERS KEEPERS! START DIGGING YOU MAY BE THE LUCKY WINNER!

In the end, the toll of the legendary blizzard was great. It totally paralyzed the East Coast from Chesapeake Bay to Maine. All communication was cut off for days. Trains and trolleys were blown off their tracks. Dozens of people were buried alive, and the storm claimed 800 lives, not counting those lost at sea, which was estimated at about 100, and those who died later from illnesses brought on by exposure. Two hundred ships were grounded. Fire stations were immobilized, and property loss was about $25 million. On average, 24 inches of snow fell on New Jersey cities. Houses were buried in snowdrifts as high as 52 feet.

Although there have been heavier snowfalls (the blizzard of 1899 brought a record 40 inches to Ocean and Burlington Counties) and there have been lower temperatures (the lowest recorded in New Jersey is thirty-four degrees below zero in Bergen County on January 5, 1904), the blizzard of 1888 goes down in history. It was documented in 1,200 personal accounts collected over the years by an organization called the Society of Blizzard Men and Blizzard Ladies of 1888. It also brought about several long-term changes in American city life.

New city ordinances put in effect the first antilitter laws; garbage and coal containers were required. Store owners were required to clean up in front of their shops. Cities had to devise detailed emergency plans in case of future snowstorms and other disasters, leading to city-controlled snow removal in most places.

Weather bureaus were affected, too. In 1891 control was taken away from the Signal Corps and handed over to the Department of Agriculture, thus creating the United States Weather Bureau. New laws required that weather bureaus stay open twenty-four hours a day, seven days a week.

Hollywood, New Jersey

· 1892 ·

When you think "lights, camera, action," you usually think Hollywood, California, with its spotlights, colorful costumes, elaborate sets, and celebrities, right? Well, when Hollywood was just an unknown town in California, the happening place to be was Fort Lee. At one time Fort Lee (originally named Fort Constitution) was the moviemaking capital of the United States—in fact, all of New Jersey was.

New York City was filled with actors and moviemaking capital, but the city was short on diversity of outdoor settings for movies. Filmmakers searched for open fields, towns with low populations, and scenic views, which they found just across the river in New Jersey. New Jersey had it all—beaches, mountains, farms, woods, and fields—all within a short distance of each other, and the towns were large enough to provide facilities such as restaurants and hotels. Word spread, and movie crews headed for Jersey in droves.

One of the locations most in demand was in the Coytesville section of Fort Lee, a place called Rambo's Roadhouse. The bottom floor of Rambo's appeared as a saloon, a hotel, a sheriff's office, and just about anything else a director's mind could muster for an Old West movie. Scores of cowboys were destined to hitch their gunbelts, plan a shoot-out, or get shot on that very front porch, while other actors were upstairs applying their makeup. Rambo's became a gathering place for anyone who was anyone in the movie business.

Fort Lee became like some kind of weird amusement park, where you could walk down the street and meet an Indian, a cowboy, a knight in armor, or a sailor. It's estimated that at one time a third of Fort Lee's population was employed by the movie studios as set people and another third was employed as extras. Everything in the town was available for rent. According to one story, a local boy asked a movie producer, "Hey, mister, you wanna rent me mudder?" The demands of the studios were endless as they released films with actors such as Douglas Fairbanks, Mary Pickford, Ethel Barrymore, Lillian Gish, and Fatty Arbuckle and by directors such as D. W. Griffith, who made over eighty films in Fort Lee.

But the movie connection to New Jersey goes back even farther than the heyday of Fort Lee. None of it would have been possible had it not been for the Wizard of Menlo Park, Thomas Alva Edison. Edison instructed his employee William K. L. Dickson to take preexisting elements, such as nitrocellulose film, clock gears, and other mechanical parts, and arrange them into a machine that enabled pictures to move. That machine was basically a cylinder installed inside a camera and coated with a light-sensitive material. Every time a picture was taken, the cylinder turned slightly and took another picture. Dickson figured out a way to add a sprocket system to the camera that would make crude film run through the viewer. Even though Dickson did the major work of turning Edison's concept into a practical reality, since he was working in Edison's lab and Edison made the important decisions, Edison ultimately took sole credit for the product.

Completed in 1892, the Edison invention, the Kinetoscope (formed from the Greek words *kineto* meaning "movement" and *scopos* meaning "to watch"), was basically a coin-operated device used by just one person to view moving pictures. The first film ever shown on the Kinetoscope was of one of Edison's workers, Fred Ott, acting out a comical sneeze, complete with a recorded sound of the sneeze that was played back with the film. People were amused when they saw it.

Realizing the moneymaking potential of moving pictures, Edison put his reputation on the line by announcing that he would show films on his new Kinetoscope at the Chicago Worlds Columbian Exposition. He needed to fill twenty-five machines with films by May of 1893. Edison decided to build the first motion-picture studio in the world, right there in West Orange, New Jersey, to fulfill his promise. He called the studio the Black Maria.

The Black Maria was a large black building constructed of wood and covered with tar paper. It had a hole in the ceiling that allowed the sun to shine through to illuminate the stage. Since changing film could take up to two hours and by then the sun would have changed position, the entire building was placed on a set of pivoting 360-degree tracks. The actors would have to go outside and pivot the building by hand to follow the sun.

Edison's reputation as an inventor and businessman per-suaded major show-business figures to travel from New York to the West Orange studio to star in his films. When the Black Maria opened its doors in December 1892, long lines of well-known vaudeville performers were on the set bright and early. They volunteered to perform free of charge in exchange for the honor of being the first subjects to appear before the Kinetoscope. Edison played on the fact that all of their egos needed to be captured on film. Each one waited patiently as the others were filmed, and then the studio was rotated for the next act to be in the spotlight.

The first performers included the strongman Eugene Sandow, the Spanish dancer Carmencita, and Annabelle Whitford performing her famous "Butterfly Dance." Also on the bill were acts from Buffalo Bill's Wild West Show such as Annie Oakley and a troupe of Native American dancers. To appeal to the male audience, some films featured scantily clad actresses, boxing, and cockfights. Edison and Dickson were thrilled and kept the film rolling.

But even with all this talent and working at a breakneck speed, the studio was unable to produce the twenty-five Kinetoscopes promised for the Chicago exposition. Instead, the first public demonstration of the machine and its finished films was at the Brooklyn Institute of Arts and Sciences on May 9, 1893. Later on, machines were placed in a row and customers were charged 25 cents for a peek.

After producing seventy-five films in two years, Edison realized that people needed more than a sneeze and a strong-man heaving and hoeing to keep them happy. So in 1896 the Black Maria produced the first film with a story line, *A Morning Alarm, Starting for the Fire and Fighting a Fire.* It was actually three short pieces, which Edison sent to the various Kinetoscopes to show. Eventually, as the public demanded more, he shot the first real narrative film, *The Great Train Robbery,* in 1903.

Once again, people gathered to watch the Edison productions. *The Great Train Robbery* lasted an entire fifteen minutes, and people were impressed. They finally saw the potential for movies and hungered for more. Word spread, and Edison's films were shown across the country in drugstores and arcades. Edison and his cronies turned out more than 2,000 films from the Black Maria, employing many circus performers, dancers, and animals.

By 1909 moviemaking was dominated by a group of thirteen manufacturers who had banded together to form the Motion Picture Patents Company, headed by Edison. Because of his patent on his movie camera, Edison had a monopoly and felt he should be paid each time someone used his Kinetoscope. He sent bill collectors to get his money. Unlicensed cameras had a way of mysteriously having "accidents" resulting in loss of negatives, equipment, buildings, and sometimes life and limb. Finally filmmakers had enough of

Edison and New Jersey. They looked elsewhere and found that the climate of California made it a good place to film movies, and it was far from Edison's reach.

Thomas Edison was the genius behind movies. He was the man responsible for making New Jersey the center of moviemaking activity—and ultimately the same person to drive it away. Eventually Edison figured "if you can't beat 'em, join 'em," and in January 1901 he closed the Black Maria and built a new glass-enclosed studio on a rooftop in New York City.

Great Balls of Fire
· 1902 ·

Although there is contradictory evidence regarding exactly how the fire got started, the most commonly told version is that shortly after midnight on the frigid night of February 9, 1902, a stove in a trolley car was not extinguished before the car was put away for the night in the storage barn of the Jersey City, Hoboken and Paterson Railway Company located between Broadway and Van Houten Street in Paterson. The car over-heated and started to burn. A local blacksmith, Charles Abrams, spotted some smoke and acted quickly. He ran to tell the night watchman, Mr. Degelman, who, in turn, ran to the nearest fire alarm box at the corner of Broadway and Main Street and pulled the lever.

Sirens blew and bells clanged as the entire firefighting force of Paterson—ninety men per shift, nine engines, and three trucks—hurried to the scene.

Although the firefighters responded as quickly as they could, heavy snow from the night before had coated the streets with a treacherous layer of ice, making it hard for the horse-drawn fire engines to move. As one of the horse-drawn carriages tried to gallop to the scene, a carriage line broke and one of the horses fell, causing the second horse to bolt and drag the first animal a few hundred yards. A firefighter named Pfitzenmeier was thrown from the carriage in the commotion, and both his legs were broken.

Added to that, gale-force winds of 40 to 60 mph lashed the

city. By the time the firemen arrived, the fire had quickly spread to neighboring buildings, often jumping blocks at a time to its next path of destruction. It hit the First Baptist Church a few blocks away, and its steeple began spitting sparks like a volcano. The firemen tried to reach the 80-foot-high steeple with the spray from their hoses, but it was of no use. Just after one o'clock in the morning, the steeple fell, crushing the church and the high school next to it. The fire continued to spread.

Further crippling their efforts was the fact that Fire Chief John Stagg was at home with pneumonia, trying to manage operations by phone. He realized that his men were seriously outmatched and by half past three had called in firefighters from the neighboring communities of Jersey City, Newark, Passaic, Clifton, Hackensack, and Ridgewood. Together the brave men stood for the next twenty-two hours, battling the greatest fire to ever hit Paterson.

Paterson at the time was the third-largest city in New Jersey and was booming with 105,271 people. Unlike the surrounding tiny suburbs, Paterson had technology such as telephones, electric lights, and trolley cars. It had more silk mills than any other city in the country. This was a major fire burning in a major city with many lives, buildings, and businesses at stake. As one eyewitness put it, "You had firebrands the size of baseballs flying all over, landing and instantly combusting other buildings. It was a wretched night."

The firemen fought with nine antiquated steam pumps that dated back to the 1870s. The fact that the firemen even answered the call was an achievement because at the time the city of Paterson was in unrest due to persistent labor disputes fueled by anarchists, and the firemen hadn't been paid in seven weeks. Thinking not of themselves, they answered the call of duty.

The fire tore into Market Street and ignited the historic Danforth Public Library on Church Street, destroying all of its records and books, a total of 37,000 volumes. Mayor John Hinchliffe himself became a hero by dragging the night watchman out of the building.

The fire continued to grow as burning debris became airborne and sparked many secondary flames.

At four o'clock the First National Bank on Ellison Street caught on fire. The flames then spread to the *Paterson Evening News* building next door, then to the YMCA. The fire did not discriminate. It tore into the 1894 French-style City Hall and into the Second National Bank building.

Then, as if to add insult to injury, the fire doubled back and shot uptown and downtown, incinerating the wood-frame buildings in its path. It consumed buildings the firemen had previously thought they'd saved. With the police station went thirty years of criminal records, including mounds of evidence for pending trials.

By five o'clock the last remnants of the library were destroyed, including two beloved statues named *Tam O'Shanter* and *Suitor Johnny* that had become legendary in poem and given status as honorary citizens. Drugstores, homes, and more businesses were consumed as the fire swept on.

Between six o'clock and noon, the Hackensack Fire Department was able to halt the fire from advancing along Sixteenth Street, but it was not over yet.

At one point, parishioners inside of St. Joseph Roman Catholic Church were listening to the morning mass, thinking the blaze was far away from them, only to learn by the end of the mass that the church's roof was on fire. Moments after the parishioners finished mass, the church was consumed in flames.

The rolling inferno finally could not advance eastward because there was open land and cemeteries blocking its path. But just to make sure, firemen made more space by dynamiting homes on Park Avenue and Carroll Street to keep the fire from spreading. Finally, by nightfall on Saturday, the worst was over.

For the next ten days, firemen sprayed the area to extinguish any burning embers beneath the rubble. Crowds came to gawk at the destruction and at the lone chimney or jagged sections of wall that remained. As the number of spectators grew into the thousands, the militia was called in to section off the area and guard bank vaults to prevent looting and further loss of treasure. Even though some safes survived the blaze, their contents sometimes suffered. If the safes weren't allowed to cool properly before they were opened, their contents could explode when hit by the sudden burst of oxygen. An order was issued to close saloons and ban beer sales for several days.

Thomas Edison brought his motion-picture camera invention to record the aftermath. The footage is today stored in the Smithsonian Institution. It was only the second fire in history to be chronicled on film.

In all, twenty-six city blocks, or eighty-four acres, were totally annihilated. Four-hundred-fifty-nine buildings were destroyed—including two city halls, the police station, a firehouse, two schools, five churches, five banks, three office buildings, a trolley barn, a theater, the library, two hotels, two newspaper plants, five clubs, and eleven leading stores—along with maps of the city that were needed when engineers tried to rebuild. In addition, in the Sandy Hill residential area, 1,000 people were left homeless. Luckily, only two people lost their lives. The fire caused $6 million in damage—which would be equivalent to $124 million today.

Even though the city of Paterson was offered condolences and financial aid from places as far away as Japan, Mayor Hinchliffe would not accept it. He stated, "Paterson can take care of its own." And they did just that. The mayor took professional contributions from Paterson bankers offering favorable terms for financing reconstruction. Architects like Fred Wesley Wentworth (who is often credited with rebuilding the city) drew up a million dollars worth of plans in less than two weeks. Within two years the city was rebuilt.

One concept that gained popularity because of the Paterson fire was that of fire departments working together. Also, firefighters worldwide learned from the fire how to prevent conflagrations—fires that jump from building to building—by routinely going to the periphery of a blaze to wet it down. Paterson passed a city ordinance stating that all buildings in the business district had to be made of brick or other fireproof materials instead of wood.

Happily, after the fire all the firemen were given their back pay, and new equipment was purchased. One of the new purchases, a 1907 steamer, was used in the movie *Ragtime* and is now on display at a Wyckoff firehouse.

The city of Paterson can proudly pat itself on the back for overcoming not only the devastation of the fire, but also a period of heavy flooding that followed later that same month. A heavy snow melted, causing nearby rivers to overflow. Nine main bridges were toppled, and the downtown area was flooded with 15 feet of water when they were just starting to rebuild.

However, through perseverance, determination, and organization, Paterson overcame Mother Nature again and survived one of the most trying years in the city's history.

When the Shark Bites

· 1916 ·

Ever since the movie *Jaws* was released, whenever people hear the word "shark," the film's ominous theme music begins to play in their heads: da na, da na. Well, believe it or not, back in 1916 the scientific community thought sharks were relatively harmless—that a shark would not attack a living person, at least not in temperate waters. Scientists felt sharks were no more dangerous than any other fish with teeth. That all changed in 1916 when one lone shark went on a killing spree during a twelve-day period in July.

It was the summer before the United States was drawn into World War I. New York City was in the throes of a deadly polio epidemic, and the East Coast was threatened by German U-boats lurking under the water. To ease the tension, Philadelphia's elite often traveled to the Long Branch section of the Jersey Shore for relaxation, while the working class of New York, New Jersey, and Pennsylvania chose other stretches of Jersey's 127-mile-long white sandy beach (from Sandy Hook to Cape May) for relief from the midsummer heat.

People at that time were just discovering the joys of swimming in the ocean. Thousands of visitors a day from New York and Pennsylvania got off the train to join New Jerseyans on the sand. The young men dressed in black tank tops and tight swim shorts that reached to their knees. Women dressed in twilled flannels with contrasting stripes and ribbons. Perhaps they hoped these costumes alone would scare off sharks!

Since sea bathing was relatively new, pamphlets were handed out that discussed what to wear and how to act on the beach: "If your teeth are of the kind which do not grow in your mouth beware lest a wave knock them out. Now bounce through the surf with a hop, skip and jump. Hold your fingers to your ears and your thumbs to your nostrils. Now dance, leap, tumble, swim, kick, float or make any motion that seems good to you."

On Saturday, July 1, Charles Vansant and his dad, a prominent doctor, and two sisters took the Number 8 train from West Philadelphia to the plush Engleside Hotel located in the upscale area of Beach Haven (named so because it was a haven from hayfever, i.e., a sneeze-free zone) to celebrate the Fourth of July weekend.

After they checked into the hotel, the young, tall, handsome, dark-haired Charles Vansant, a promising graduate student, headed to the beach. On his way to the surf, he befriended a large Chesapeake Bay retriever and waved to his summertime friend, Alexander Ott, a lifeguard who had been a member of the prestigious American Olympic swim team.

Vansant waded into the ocean with the playful dog and then decided to go for a swim beyond the lifelines into chest-deep water, calling the animal to follow him. The dog, however, had other plans and headed back to shore. Vansant kept calling it, hoping to change its mind. Meanwhile, as Vansant was busily trying to convince the dog, a small group of people on shore noticed a dark shadow lingering just beneath the surf.

All of a sudden, a black fin sliced through the water and headed toward Vansant. The people on shore started to shout, but Vansant was busy calling for the dog. He was only 50 yards from the shore when his dog calling turned into a high-pitched shriek. He started to splash frantically and tried to swim toward shore. The water around him turned a sickening red.

Vansant managed to make it 10 yards and was now in only 3½ feet of water. Lifeguard Ott darted across the beach and, without thinking of his own life, dived in to rescue Vansant. The shark clung onto its meal; it did not let Vansant go until its belly scraped the bottom, as one eyewitness recalled.

Two local residents, John Everton and Sheridan Taylor, locked arms and created a human chain to help Ott drag Vansant out of the water. As Vansant lay sprawled on the beach, blood flowed out of him. All the flesh from his left thigh had been stripped away to the hipbone. There was also a large gash on his right leg. His sister Louise stood frozen in horror as she watched the life drain from her brother.

Thinking quickly, Ott grabbed the skirt of one of the female bathers to make a tourniquet. Vansant's dad, Dr. Eugene Vansant, a nose and throat physician, along with a medical student who had been on the beach, carried Vansant to the hotel and cleared a large wooden desk to create a bed. They tried to stop the bleeding. Another doctor, a Dr. Willis, was called to the scene to assist, but it was to no avail. Charles Vansant was pronounced dead at 6:45 P.M. The official cause of death was "hemorrhage from femoral artery, left side" and "bitten by a shark while bathing."

New Jersey and Philadelphia reacted to the Vansant attack with utter horror. It was the first fatal shark attack ever recorded on the East Coast. The *New York Times,* however, practically dismissed the incident, putting just a small article on page eighteen: "Dies After Attack By Fish . . . Presumably a Shark." After all, the polio epidemic left kids dying at the rate of one per hour—this seemed trivial.

New Jersey newspapers tried to keep the event quiet. No one wanted to lose business over the Fourth of July weekend. To reassure bathers, Robert Engle, the owner of the Engleside resort, put up protective netting near the surf, 300 feet from the shoreline and extending the entire length of the beach.

With the nets in place, people felt safe. By July 6, just five days after the attack, people were back splashing in the ocean. Even though no one spoke of the attack, pools were a lot more crowded than usual, and rescue boat patrols were on the lookout for dorsal fins.

The next attack happened at Spring Lake, 45 miles north of Beach Haven. Spring Lake was one of the summer hot spots for the rich and famous. One of the hotels of choice was the Essex and Sussex, called the E&S for short. On staff on the fateful July day were two well-liked men, Bruder, a bell captain and excellent swimmer, and Nolan, an elevator operator. They were forced to work during the incredible heat, so they took their regular lunch break at 1:45 P.M. to go for a quick ocean swim. Also on staff were two lifeguards, White and Anderson.

Bruder and Nolan joined some of their friends in the employee swimming area. Bruder enjoyed the force of the ocean and swam far beyond the lifeline boundaries. When Bruder's friends left to dry off, he stayed to swim a little longer. Apparently, he didn't hear the theme song.

He screamed. The lifeguards realized that there was a man out there struggling for his life in the ocean. White and Anderson hopped into a lifeboat.

Bruder's body was flung into the air between bites. His screams were ear-piercing. One woman, a classic socialite widow, Mona Childs, watched the whole thing through her theater glasses. She saw the shark turn away then dart back at him "just as an airplane attacks a zeppelin." Mrs. Childs contacted the hotel switchboard operator and sent an urgent message to her niece, who was on the Jersey Shore elsewhere, and to other hotels, "Get out of the water!" It took only twelve minutes to clear the water from Spring Lake to Cape May.

As the lifeguards approached Bruder, he yelled, "A shark bit me! Bit off my legs!" White extended an oar, but the weakened Bruder couldn't grab it. He held out his arms, pleading for help. The two lifeguards pulled Bruder's body into the lifeboat. Both legs had been severed at the knees. Bruder turned pale and went into shock. The lifeguards watched in horror as the life drained from his severed body. The shark had claimed its second victim.

The whole scene was witnessed from shore by hundreds of tourists, many from the upper crust of society. A doctor from the E&S hotel was there to examine the body, but he was asked to first take care of the women who had fainted and vomited on shore.

This time the media paid attention. Scientists at the American Museum in Manhattan and other experts of the day could no longer claim that sharks didn't attack people. Three leading shark experts held a press conference: Dr. Lucas (an anatomist), Robert Murphy (a zoologist), and Dr. Nichols (a true ichthyologist). All greatly stressed the unlikelihood of another attack, but they did mention that a ¾-inch-thick steel-wire-mesh fence, like the one up at Asbury Park, wasn't a bad idea either. Some reporters asked if the attacker could be something other than a shark. Some chimed in, "How about a killer mackerel, monstrous sea turtles, or maybe even the German U-boats?" And they were serious!

Dr. Schauffler, the surgeon general of the New Jersey National Guard who examined Bruder's wounds and who later became a major figure in the New Jersey Medical Society and a huge proponent for wire mesh in ocean swimming areas, stated, "There is not the slightest doubt that a man-eating shark inflicted these injuries." Despite this statement, seasoned seamen and other "experts" were quoted as saying, "It was a freak accident, and it couldn't happen again in a thousand years."

To save the season, the headlines in the *Asbury Park Press* proclaimed, "Nets and armed motorboats to protect bathers. . . . Believed precaution taken will assure absolute safety to bathers along the north shore."

Once again, people flocked to the waters. Boats went out armed with rifles, axes, harpoon guns, and long lines of sheep guts to bait the sharks. Several brave souls planned to lure in and kill the man-eating beast.

On July 8, in the swimming area at Asbury Park, a lifeguard captain spotted a shark just outside the swim ropes. He was forced to beat this 12-foot-long beast with an oar. After enough cracks on the head, the shark fled. The story made the front pages, and soon every testosterone gland in the state was itching to fend off its own shark. Many sharks were captured and shot. Cartoonists had a field day depicting politicians and U-boats as sharks and saying that the female bathing suit was the only shark-proof needed. Beach locations chose a different angle and advertised "Come down and laugh at the captured sharks we have enclosed in our bathing area with enforced nets."

By July 12 the shark excitement had died down. The media focus had shifted to Pancho Villa and his Mexican bandits. Swimming attendance was once again up. This time the attack setting was a quaint little business town of only 1,200 people, 30 miles north of Spring Lake and 16 miles inland from the sea, called Matawan. The town was so small that the head cop was also the town barber.

Even though Matawan was inland, it had one obscure serpentine connection to the Atlantic Ocean, a transport route for farm produce known as Matawan Creek. It was a narrow, winding passage only about 40 feet across at its widest point and only 30 feet deep.

On the afternoon of the 12th, Captain Thomas Cottrell was returning from the nearby fishing grounds when he spotted a dark gray shape about 8 feet in length making its way west up the creek with the incoming tide. He knew it was a shark. He had seen them many times before in the open sea. He looked up and saw four drawbridge workers staring at the same thing. Cottrell raced into town and tried to reach the town barber/chief of police, but he was shrugged off as simply reacting to the shark panic that had swept the state. Cottrell didn't give up. He knew what he had seen. He ran to the barbershop and to other businesses, but everyone laughed at him. "You have a better chance seeing an elephant cooling off down there than a shark," they taunted. No one could believe a saltwater shark would make its way up a creek, 16 miles away from the ocean.

Frustrated, Cottrell drove to the creek to warn any swimmers. Unfortunately, he ran past the dock area just seconds before a group of local boys arrived for their afternoon swim.

Lester Stillwell enjoyed swimming in the buff in the muddy waters of Matawan Creek. Lester had the "fits," which today is known as epilepsy, and often would shake with unconscious, violent convulsions. The kids knew to watch out for Lester. The boys played tag in the water, totally unaware of the warning Cottrell was shouting around town.

One of the kids, Ally O'Hara, felt a sandpaper-like object graze his leg. He looked into the water and saw the tail of a huge fish. Lester was right near him in the shallow water, but before Ally could say anything, Lester had made his way to one of the deep pools and was floating on his back. "Hey, fellas, watch me float." But most of the boys were busy watching a kid named Anthony trying to make a fancy dive. At the same time Anthony dived into the water, they heard a short scream and a big splash behind them. They saw what looked like an old board behind Lester, and then in a second they saw the dorsal and tail fins of the shark. They shouted, "Lester's gone." At that moment they saw Lester again, this time in the mouth of the shark. Lester tried to scream, but his mouth was filled with water, and all the boys heard was a gurgle before their friend was dragged underneath the surface. The muddy water turned crimson red. The boys flew out of the water and headed straight for the main street of town screaming, "Shark! Shark! A shark got Lester!" They were still naked.

Still, no one believed it was a shark; some thought the boys were pranking. One man, Stanley Fisher, thought that Lester might have had one of his epileptic fits. He grabbed some locals and headed toward the creek. "If we don't grab Lester soon, he'll be finished."

By the time they got to the dock, almost half an hour had passed since Lester was attacked. They realized he was probably dead. The townspeople gathered by the creek. There was a strange redness to the water. One man brought some chicken wire and hooks from his hardware store, and they hung a fence down from a nearby train trestle to trap the boy's body so it wouldn't be swept out to sea. They did not realize that by doing this, they were also trapping the shark inside.

Three men, George Burlew, Stanley Fisher, and Arthur Smith, decided to dive into the creek and attempt to find the boy's body. When fifty-one-year-old Smith dived, he scraped his stomach against a moving object. After he came to the surface, he saw that his stomach was bleeding from the encounter.

Fisher dived to the bottom and thought he saw a log rolling on top of Lester's body. The muddy water made it hard to tell. As Fisher surfaced, Burlew noticed a weird swirl of water around him. The men looked at each other and decided they needed to get out of the creek. Then Fisher caught sight of Lester's mom crying, so he decided to give it one more try. He took a deep breath and dived down to the muddy creek bed and again saw the log moving near the boy's body. He tugged at the body and was able to dislodge it.

Fisher stood in waist-deep water holding Lester's body. Suddenly a mighty force rammed into his right leg. The force swirled him around. He dropped Lester's remains and shouted, "He's got me! The shark's got me!"

The man fought with every ounce of his strength—punching, kicking, and pushing at the monster he couldn't see. A boat raced toward him. Arthur Van Buskirk, the deputy sheriff, struck the shark several times with his oar. Finally, after a violent game of tug-of-war, the shark let go. The shark left Fisher's thighbone exposed with blood spurting in every direction.

A doctor raced to Fisher's side but was not sure what to do

with this long jagged wound. He quickly tied a big rubber band around the severed leg, but the band broke. Then he applied a regular tourniquet. No doctor in America, prior to the past few days, had ever seen a wound like this. A stretcher was improvised for Fisher, and arrangements were urgently arranged for a train to skip all its normal stops and take him to the closest hospital, Monmouth Memorial.

As the town was preoccupied with saving Fisher, the shark was worried about its own hide. It broke through the makeshift wire fence and headed out to sea. This unpredictable man-eater wasn't done dining. It ignored all the logic and science of the day and headed to its next meal just a half mile east of Matawan.

The next victim was twelve-year-old Joseph Dunn. Joseph and his brother, Michael, were swimming on the north bank of Matawan Creek when they heard someone nearby yelling "Shark!" Michael made it to shore and spun around when he heard a powerful splash and a shriek. He turned to see where his brother was and noticed Joseph's head bobbing up and down about 10 feet from the dock. Joseph fought desperately, trying to avoid being tugged under. The water started to turn red. Several boys ran for help while Michael and his friend Jerry tried to reach Joseph. Michael dived back in the water and grabbed Joseph's hand. He pulled and pulled, determined to save his brother, but he was no match for the powerful shark. Just as the shark was dragging Joseph under again, a hand rushed up behind the two boys and jerked Joseph out of the mouth of the shark. That hand belonged to Robert Thress, a bricklayer who happened to be in the area.

They all got to the nearby dock ladder just as Captain Cottrell, the first man to spot the shark, cruised up in his motorboat. They told Cottrell what had just happened. Cottrell took Joseph into his boat and quickly sped him to the crew that had treated Fisher.

The front and side portions of Joseph's legs were torn like

ribbons, but luckily no arteries had been severed. He had a better chance of survival than Fisher, so they decided to transfer him by car to the hospital. As the boy was being put in the car, newspaper reporters asked him, "How did it feel?" Joseph, still numb and unable to feel the pain, said, "As if the shark was trying to swallow my whole leg." He refused to tell the reporters his name and address for fear his mother would find out before he got a chance to tell her he was all right.

Stanley Fisher had lost too much blood by the time he reached the hospital. His last words were "I found the boy on the bottom. I got Lester away from the shark; anyhow, I did my duty." Young Joseph Dunn was the lone survivor of the shark attacks, though he needed several skin grafts on his legs.

The townspeople of Matawan were outraged. They were determined to get this beast. It had killed one of their own. They believed the shark would return to the scene of the crime at high tide, and they waited with full artillery. They had dynamite, pitchforks, shotguns, harpoons, rifles, garden hoses, axes, ice picks, and hammers. Some even hung legs of lambs off the train trestle to lure the shark out. But they had a huge challenge. Sharks are among the most perfect predators and efficient killers in the sea. Their multiple rows of teeth shred a victim. They can detect the slightest vibration from up to 1,000 feet away. They posses unique organs that allow them to detect a personal electrical field. They are sensitive to light contrasts, so something as simple as tan lines or the soles of one's feet can provoke an attack. They can detect one part blood mixed with twenty million parts water. They are also attracted to odors such as feces, garbage, and vomit. Truly, they are creatures to be reckoned with.

The mayor of Matawan issued a $100 reward for sharks dead or alive. Nationwide headlines read "Armed posses comb the coast to snuff out man-eating shark." The shark attacks outpressed the impending war. The U.S. Coast Guard, National Marine Fisheries Service, and federal agents were called in to organize a battle against the man-eater. The House of Representatives appropriated $5,000 to eradicate the Jersey Shore of the threat of sharks. Every shark was considered the enemy. People went on a shark-killing spree, with hundreds being killed each day.

Scientists were frustrated and baffled. These attacks went contrary to everything they believed about sharks. The head ichthyologist of the time, Dr. Nichols, believed the culprit was one lone shark—a great white shark—who had strayed thousands of miles from home. It turned out he was right.

While professionals, seamen, and novices were shooting, spearing, netting, and capturing any shark they saw, two men, forty-five-year-old Michael Schleisser, a chief animal trainer for the Barnum and Bailey Circus and a top taxidermist for several national museums, and his friend, Robert Murphy, decided to travel up the creek to Matawan. They borrowed a friend's motorboat, departed from South Amboy, and headed to Raritan Bay for a few hours. Before they left the dock, Schleisser accidentally broke one of the two wooden boat oars but decided to bring it along for the ride. The men had no idea what was in store.

Near Sandy Hook, only a few miles from the mouth of Matawan Creek, the men dropped a dragnet from the stern to catch some panfish for breakfast. As their craft sputtered along, suddenly a tremendous jerk pulled the boat and stalled the engine. Schleisser looked over the stern to see what the problem was. He spotted the problem all right—it was a big black tail fin! "My God, we've got a shark!"

The shark became increasingly violent in its attempt to free itself from the net. Schleisser looked down—the shark was as big as the boat! In desperation and with the will for survival, he grabbed the broken oar and jammed it into the head of the shark. He pounded its gills, its nose—anything he could reach—with the oar. The more he pounded the shark, the angrier it became and the more it entangled itself in the net. At one point, the shark's teeth caught Schleisser in the elbow, but he kept pounding the shark with every ounce of strength he could muster, and finally the shark let go. When the shark lay still, the two men signaled a larger boat to help them. They hitched the shark to the side of the larger boat and hauled it to a dock in Atlantic Highlands and then back to South Amboy.

The fishermen who helped lift the shark onto the dock sensed there was something different about it than the hundreds of others hauled in during the shark mania. Instead of hanging this one upside down for display, Schleisser and Murphy decided to open up the shark to see the contents of its digestive tract. Spectators gathered.

Schleisser, using his taxidermic skills, firmly held the knife and plunged the tip of the sharp blade just short of the chest region. One grasp with his hands and he knew the intestines had questionable contents. As he was about to make the final cut to reveal its contents, a dentist who had been watching this event suggested he wait until medical personnel were available to identify the remains. Schleisser agreed, and soon the dentist returned with two physician friends. The doctors found human tissue in the shark's digestive track as well as a human rib and the 11-inch shinbone of a boy.

They had found their killer: a single dull blue great white shark with a white belly and a mouth that, when open, could fit a man's head inside. It had four rows of teeth, was 7½ feet in length, and weighed 350 pounds.

By the afternoon of Wednesday, July 19, Schleisser had stuffed the shark and opened an exhibit of his man-eater at the *Bronx Home News* building. Thirty thousand people lined up to catch a glimpse of the sea monster. Schleisser and Murphy retold the chilling story of its final minutes.

This is the first and only known case of a serial shark killer in the world. Although there was no definitive proof that one shark was responsible for all of the killings, the attacks stopped after the Schleisser catch, and it was the only shark found to contain human remains.

Terrorist Attack
Blamed on
Mosquitoes
· 1916 ·

On the Jersey side of New York Harbor, opposite the Statue of Liberty, there was once an island called Black Tom, named after a fisherman who was at one time the island's sole inhabitant. The Central Railroad of New Jersey purchased the site as a storage area and enlarged it by filling in a strip of land from the mainland to the island so their railroad cars could get across.

By July of 1916 the island was bustling with activity. It was now owned by a subsidiary of the Central Railroad, the National Dock and Storage Company, and served as a depot for tons of munitions and explosive powders, with cargo destined for England, Russia, and France, America's allies in the Great War. Seventy-five percent of all munitions and armaments sent from the United States to Europe left from the New York/New Jersey area, and most of it came from the "Arsenal of Democracy," Black Tom Island. The only place where there was more ammunition was at the European war front itself.

At the time, America was still neutral. President Woodrow Wilson adamantly wanted to keep the peace and go down in history as the president who "kept us out of war." Wilson was also preoccupied with two other things: the death of his wife and the disturbances in Mexico.

Even though eighty fully armed German ships were settled in the neutral waters of the Hudson River for the duration of the war, Americans felt confident that the Atlantic Ocean would keep the war away from them. The average American citizen just wanted to work and enjoy the fruits of his or her labor. Those in New Jersey wanted to take their minds off the recent shark attacks and the outbreak of infantile paralysis (polio) that was affecting their New York neighbors.

By everyone's standards, July 29, 1916, was just a normal Saturday. That night people settled in their homes. The longshoremen, having completed their normal six-day work week, went home, leaving nearly a hundred freight cars waiting to be unloaded. The cars contained between two and four million pounds of explosives, from small arms to deadly TNT in bulk. In addition to the explosives on the island, there was also a barge, the *Johnson,* moored tight against one of the piers, Pier 17, in direct violation of New Jersey safety laws. This vessel held 100,000 pounds of TNT and 417 cases of detonating fuses.

Considering all this ammunition, the island was poorly guarded. There were no gates or guardhouses, and security regulations were readily ignored. Left on the island that night was the usual Sunday skeleton crew of six railroad detectives and two additional detectives from a private agency to watch the labyrinth of warehouses, boxcars, and explosives. The only other inhabitants on the island at the time were the infamous Jersey mosquitoes, who attacked the eight men unmercifully during the night. On previous occasions the guards had lit smudge pots, which was against regulations, to ward off the millions of blood-sucking insects.

Then, at twelve minutes past midnight, everything began to change. One of the detectives, Barton Scott, noticed a fire on the *Johnson* in Pier 17. "I ran to a telephone and called for the yard engines to come and pull the other [train] cars away, and within a few minutes after the discovery of the fire, shrapnel shells of the smaller calibers began to explode." As the fire got hotter, the explosives went off with increasing violence.

At 12:40 A.M. a fire alarm attached to a sprinkler in one of the warehouses signaled the Jersey City Fire Department, and three engines came to the scene. Firemen quickly aimed their hoses at the potential inferno. The streams of water shot out and just barely licked the violent flames. It was as if the water was serving as fuel rather than a deterrent. The firemen worked feverishly for the next hour and a half as a handful of people watched.

Then, at 2:08 A.M., all hell broke loose. A thunderous blast filled the night air. "A million people, maybe five million, were awakened by an explosion that shook the houses along the marshy Jersey shores, rattled the skyscrapers on the foundations of Manhattan, threw people from their beds miles away and sent terror broadcast," reported the *New York Times*.

The huge explosion lit up the night sky, sending shock waves that pounded on areas as far as 100 miles away, from New York to Maryland.

In Manhattan windows shattered, sending thousands of glass splinters speeding through the air and plunging to the streets below like daggers. Those out on the streets were knocked to the ground, and people were thrown from their beds. A ten-week-old boy in Jersey City, Arthur Tosson, was hurled from his crib to his death.

Subway cars shook, frightening the passengers onboard. Underground cargo railway tubes connecting lower Manhattan with Hoboken and Jersey City were jolted, as those conductors still inside feared for their lives, expecting the water to burst through.

Then the night became eerily quiet. People popped their heads out of their windows to see what had happened. Suddenly the bombardment resumed. People assumed the United States was under attack from some invisible enemy.

Thousands ran into the streets, women rushed out of hotels half dressed, people became hysterical, and police whistles were blown frantically—but even the police themselves didn't know who was behind the attack.

Blasts kept coming, and the chaos continued. Burglar alarms went off, storefront plate-glass windows shattered, all the phone lines in New York and Jersey City went dead, and ambulances from every hospital in Manhattan and Jersey City were dispatched. At first some thought the explosion had happened in the financial district in Manhattan, but then they realized it was coming from Black Tom Island in Jersey City.

As the fire swept from cargo to cargo of deadly explosives, shock waves kept pounding the area. One policeman told of how he was thrown several yards into the air, and when he returned to consciousness, he saw that his shoes had been blown off and his cap was in ribbons.

The Brooklyn Bridge swayed at the impact of the waves, leaving motorists terrified as their windshields exploded. People in houseboats and barges below were thrown overboard.

In Jersey City the ceilings of the courtroom and the assembly chamber in City Hall were wrecked, and nearly every window and glass door in the building was broken. The great stained-glass windows in St. Patrick's Church, considered the finest building in Jersey City, were destroyed. At City Hospital the patients had to be moved away from exploding windows. Prisoners incarcerated in Hackensack feared for their lives, for they had nowhere to run. Even those long dead in the graveyards were jolted as their tombstones toppled and the vaults were thrown out of whack.

The explosions kept coming every twenty minutes or so. Shrapnel pellets ripped through the Statue of Liberty, but luckily her torch remained lit. Using that light, police heroically transported some of the Statue of Liberty staff workers, who lived on Bedloe's Island, to the safety of Governors Island. In total they moved twelve women and thirteen children.

Two big barges filled with ammunition were blown from their berths and were now ablaze, floating down the river and firing at will like crazed banshees with machine guns. The *New York World Telegram* wrote, "They drifted toward Ellis Island, where five hundred immigrants, fleeing war's terrors in Europe, cowered." A mass evacuation of Ellis Island transported the hysterical immigrants from the immigration center to the Battery at the southern tip of Manhattan, where police guarded them to make sure no one sneaked away.

Meanwhile, tugboats, New York fireboats, and Coast Guard cutters went into the line of fire and tried to pour water onto the floating infernos. The explosions continued for several hours.

As daylight approached, people watched dumbstruck as black smoke billowed from Black Tom Island and rolled over the water. Hundreds of New Jersey Hospital volunteers went to the island to try to help whatever victims there might be.

When the explosions finally ended, the devastation was immense. Several bodies washed ashore. Hundreds of people who were near the site were seriously injured, and hundreds more were hurt by the shock waves and fallout. Millions of windows were broken in New York and New Jersey, and Black Tom Island itself was a burnt-out hollow with holes so deep in the land that some went below sea level. Thirteen huge ware-houses that had held food supplies were leveled, six piers were destroyed, and hundreds of railroad cars and barges were blown apart. The estimated damage was $20 million. The *New York Times* wrote, "Destruction more complete than was created on Black Tom would be hard to imagine."

Miraculously not a single person on the streets of New York or Jersey City was injured by the shattered glass, only one looting occurred, and none of the firemen on Black Tom Island were killed. "Firemen, blackened by smoke, and their clothing torn to tatters, came staggering out of the smoke, but they were too dazed to tell what had happened," reported the *Times*. The next few days were filled with talk of the heroic efforts of the firemen.

As controllable fires continued to burn, thoughts turned to who was to blame. The first assumption was that it had been an accident, with the railroads and storage companies at fault. Arrests were made, and manslaughter charges were brought against the companies. But as the year unfolded, pieces of evidence started to emerge and point a finger at the real villains: the Germans, with the German ambassador to the United States, Count Johann Von Bernstorff, as the ringmaster working from his Washington, D.C., office. His dual mission was to keep President Wilson and thus the U.S. from entering World War I so we wouldn't fight against the Germans, while at the same time overseeing Germany's terrorist plots against America on her own soil.

With a ring of sabotage spies at his disposal and orders coming from Section 3B of German military intelligence, the Germans managed, under Von Bernstorff's leadership, to pull off 200 acts of terrorism on the United States, twenty-eight of which took place in New York and New Jersey. Starting in January 1915 with the blowing up of the Roebling wire and cable plant in Trenton to bombing the Senate Chamber of the Capitol building in Washington, D.C. (where several people were killed), to blowing up the Kingsland ammunition plant in New Jersey, to the sinking of the *Lusitania* in neutral waters with innocent Americans onboard, to injecting horses and mules that were going to be transported to the allies with anthrax, to hiding glass-tube devices inside pencils that would explode once snapped, to "cigar" bombs that were placed on ships and would explode hours after they went out to sea, to messages written in invisible ink and manuals written with protocol on how the terrorists should act to blend in socially with the Americans, and continuing with other small acts of terror, the Germans secretly attacked America. Their actions were revealed in a letter the British decoded—with the help of three "acquired" German code manuals that no one knew the British had until after the war—called the Zimmerman letter. The letter was named after its author, Arthur Zimmerman, an undersecretary to some head honcho in Berlin, who was trying to get Mexico and Japan to start a war against the United States.

The deciphered Zimmerman letter was addressed to Ambassador Von Bernstorff and established that Germany's attacks on neutral America were routed through him. The letter not only gave names and addresses of who he could trust to carry out sabotage in the United States and Canada, but it went on to specify just what acts of terrorism he should carry out: "In the U.S. sabotage can be carried out in every kind of factory for supplying munitions of war. Railway embankments and bridges must not be touched. Embassy must in no circumstances be compromised. Similar precautions must be taken in regard to Irish pro-German propaganda." Shortly after receiving the letter, on April 2, 1917, with only $11,000 in its defense budget, America entered the war. However, the discovery of the letter was poorly timed, because just twenty days earlier, on February 4, the United States had broken relations with Germany because of its unrestricted submarine warfare and sent Von Bernstorff home. Thus the U.S. government was never able to prosecute him.

It wasn't until twenty-three years after World War II, armed with 1,032 cubic feet of documents, that American officials were able to completely unravel and prove the case against Germany. There were no witnesses, and the Germans denied responsibility for the attacks. At one point when the Americans were closing in on the case, the Germans claimed that the entire explosion at Black Tom Island had been caused by the Jersey mosquitoes. They produced a witness who claimed he saw a night watchman start a fire on Black Tom that night to "drive away the mosquitoes." The claim was disproved, and cartoonists and newspapers had a field day with the fact that

Germany tried to blame the attack on mosquitoes.

Finally, in April 1935 a hired historian in an Austrian archive found a large volume of German material that specifically mentioned the Kingsland fire and other munitions-plant explosions and fires in the New York area. Investigators had their smoking gun. A worldwide manhunt spanning Europe, North and South America, and Asia ensued to bring to justice most of the players in the worst terrorist attack to hit the U.S. mainland up to that time. (All of this is elaborately detailed in Jules Witcover's book, *Sabotage at Black Tom: Imperial Germany's Secret War in America, 1914–1917.*) Although it was firmly established that the Germans did the deed, the exact details of that fateful night have died with the perpetrators.

It is known that a large part of the planning for these sabotage operations happened at a town house in Manhattan at 123 West Fifteenth Street, which was owned by a former German opera singer named Martha Held. German sailors whose ships had been interned in New York Harbor at the start of the war met there, pretending it was a recreation center. Those who lived in the neighborhood thought it was a brothel.

The most likely scenario for the Black Tom Island attack is this: Lothar Witzke, a German seaman whose ship had been interned and who was recruited for the Black Tom mission, and Kurt Jahnke, a German-born naturalized American citizen and former U.S. marine who directed West Coast sabotage operations, went to Black Tom in a small boat laden with explosives on timed fuses. Around midnight they pulled up to Pier 17, where the *Johnson* was tied. Meanwhile, Michael Kristoff, an immigrant drifter looking to make a few extra bucks, arrived on Black Tom via land. All three set fires in a couple of the boxcars containing TNT and planted bombs at various pier locations. Then Jahnke and Witzke went out into the river to watch their handiwork.

After the incident Witzke and Jahnke vanished, leaving Kristoff as the prime suspect at the time. Before anyone realized it was a terrorist act, the New Jersey police arrested Kristoff as an arson suspect, but the case against him was too weak. He was let go and the leads went dead for a while. Eventually Witzke got caught and Kristoff was arrested again, this time on suspected sabotage charges. Witzke was convicted in a Texas military court and sentenced to hang. He was the only man thus sentenced in the United States during World War I, but President Wilson, ever the pacifist, changed his sentence to life in prison. Kristoff was jailed, then released, and later died of tuberculosis in Staten Island Hospital. Jahnke went on to become the sole naval confidential agent for Germany in Mexico and acted in that capacity till the end of the war. He was never punished for his role in Black Tom.

After years of pursuing a case against Germany, Americans were ultimately victorious with an award of $50 million in restitution for acts of war. The final payments were made in 1979, sixty-three years after the acts of sabotage were done. By then, many of the principals in the case were dead.

Ironically the one surviving principal was John J. McCloy, the prosecutor who assumed the lead in the investigation and got the case reopened after the Americans had already lost twice in front of the Mixed Claims Committee. After winning the Black Tom and Kingsland case by proving Imperial Germany's involvement, he served as an advisor to every president from Franklin Roosevelt to Ronald Reagan, and he later had an office in the World Trade Center with a clear view of where Black Tom Island once stood, eighty-five years ago.

Little did he know that he was in the very towers where history would repeat itself. As the *Washington Post* noted back in October of 1941, three days after the final victory decision, "These explosions occurred so long ago that their memory, and also their moral seem rather dim and distant today, yet history repeats and its lessons are often highly instructive. This reminder of German government techniques . . . is not to be overlooked."

Today Liberty State Park stands on the rebuilt ruins of Black Tom Island. Few people there would even suspect that they are standing on the site of the first major terrorist attack on the U.S. mainland. Even more haunting is that from that very site, they can peer back at Manhattan and remember a mass grave caused by yet another terrorist attack, where the mighty Twin Towers once stood.

Under the River and through the Woods
· 1920 ·

The idea of building a stone tube under the Hudson River for easier access for motorists traveling between New York and New Jersey was first suggested in the nineteenth century by a Hoboken man named John Stevens who was frustrated with the delays and unreliability of the ferry services. He was ignored because his suggestion was considered impossible.

But the problems with the ferries—the only way to get across the Hudson at the time—grew worse. The ferries were originally built to carry horses and carriages, not automobiles. As a result, only a few cars could be carried on each trip, causing a several-hour wait just to take the thirty-minute ride. The problem really hit home when a seven-day winter storm froze the Hudson and caused a food shortage in Manhattan. Something had to be done.

A bistate committee was formed in 1919, and after studying various options, guess what? They decided that building a tunnel wasn't such a bad idea after all. They briefly thought about building a bridge as an option, but that idea was ruled out because of how high the bridge would have to be for boats to pass under. So a tunnel it was. First, they had to figure out a way to dig nearly 2 miles down below the surface of the Hudson to get to bedrock. Second, they had to devise a way to circulate air in a tunnel that deep. And third, they had to come up with a way to get rid of the deadly carbon monoxide fumes that would be in the tunnel. In short, this tunnel posed more problems than any other tunnel that had been built in the world up to that time.

The committee recommended General W. Goethals to spearhead the project. After all, he was the guy who had built the Panama Canal—surely he would be the man to carry out the job. But another engineer, Clifford M. Holland, a thirty-six-year-old civil engineer and Harvard graduate who happened to be an employee of the New York State Bridge and Tunnel Commission and of the New Jersey Interstate Bridge and Tunnel Commission got wind of the project and came up with a well-thought-out plan. Since the tunnel is named after him, it's not hard to figure out who got the job.

On July 1, 1919, Holland became the chief engineer at a whopping salary of $12,000 a year. He beat out Goethals by coming up with the idea to build smaller-sized twin tubes lined with both cast iron and concrete for industrial strength, rather than the single large concrete bilevel tube that Goethals suggested.

Holland was no newcomer to the field. He had worked on both the Battery and the East River tunnel projects and was recognized as a leader in his field. And the fact was, tunnels under the Hudson were not a new thing—there was already a rail tunnel that had been opened in 1910. It was the size of this project, and the fact that it would be carrying motorists, that was new. This tunnel project would require some serious "outside the box" thinking to make the tunnel safe.

At the time, emissions tests on cars were unheard of. However, Holland could think of no other way to know what he was dealing with than to see how much fumes each car produced and consequently how much carbon monoxide would be in the tunnel.

To find this out, he put different cars inside an abandoned Pittsburgh coal mine and turned them on to see how much carbon monoxide each emitted. To measure these levels, he sat volunteer Yale students, who were willing to inhale the mixture of air and carbon monoxide, inside the cars then tested their blood to see the effects. The results: Air with only one-half percent of carbon monoxide is lethal.

After the results were in, he built a miniature tunnel and then started work on the air circulation challenge. He worked around the clock with his team to figure out how to funnel fresh air into the tunnel. He worked until he had a solution.

In the end he designed a totally new system of ventilation. He called it a "vertical transverse flow." The main component of the system was big fans. How big? Eighty feet in diameter, or the size of a ten-story building! It was basically a twin-duct system using eighty-four powerful electric fans (forty-two blowing and forty-two exhaust) that would pump 3,600,000 cubic feet of fresh air per minute into the tunnel. Fans would blow fresh air in and then force it out through vents in the curbing into chambers beneath the roadway. At that point, that air would mix with the exhaust fumes and rise to the ceiling, and the dirty air would be pushed out. The whole process took ninety seconds. Ironically, the air inside the tunnel would be purer than the air outside the tunnel. The system would use 6,000 total horsepower, and the power was arranged in four ventilation buildings to be located on both ends of the tunnel.

On October 12, 1920, a ground-breaking ceremony was held in New York. A few days later, construction began on the Jersey side. Crews on both sides worked at a feverish pace. On a good day they could blast through almost 15 feet, hoping to soon connect in the middle. They had some serious digging to do. The length of the tunnel, portal to portal, was 8,558 feet for the north tube and 8,371 feet for the south tube. The width of the roadway would be 20 feet, with a total of four lanes.

The underwater job was tricky. Water had to be held back in special pressurized excavation chambers to prevent it from rushing in so the men could work. Many workers suffered from the bends (residual nitrogen in the blood from being under pressurized water).

After years of around-the-clock work with barely any sleep, Holland broke down. On October 8, 1924, he took a vacation due to "continued devotion, night and day, during the past five years." He figured he would rest for one month so he would be in great shape for the historical "holing through"— the day when both sides of the underwater tunnel would meet. He never made it. He died of exhaustion, suffering a heart attack on October 27, 1924, the eve of the holing through.

With the creator and chief engineer of the project dead, the special celebration that was planned was postponed. Holland never got to see his finished tunnel. Strangely, neither did his successor, who also died of exhaustion five months after taking the job.

Two days after Holland's death, it was decided that he would have wanted them to continue, so President Calvin Coolidge pushed a button in Washington to "set off" the final explosion. The New York and New Jersey crews shook hands in the middle of the tunnel.

After seven years of construction, thirteen lives lost on the job, and $48 million spent, on November 12, 1927, New Jersey governor Harry Moore and Jersey City mayor Frank Hague opened the world's first long underwater mechanically venti-lated vehicular tunnel. New York representatives were there as well. There was a dedication ceremony, and for the next sev-eral hours, people (20,000 in just the first hour!) walked through the tunnel from one side to the other. Everyone was cheerful and in awe of this engineering feat. These people's lives had now been made much easier, their travel time to work much less. People shouted and sang through the New Jersey streets. They knelt down to breathe in the fresh air flowing through the tunnel. Entrepreneurs were already planning the opening of several tunnelside diners.

Then, at the stroke of midnight, the tunnel was closed to

pedestrians forever. A few minutes after midnight, honking cars rumbled through. The first driver through from the Jersey side (not counting officials, of course) was Frank Finn, an attorney. He had waited patiently for several hours to be the first in the long line of traffic to go through the tunnel and pay his 50-cent toll. A thousand cars—seven across, four blocks deep—waited on the Jersey side ready to take their turn through this modern-day wonder. It was a trip they could tell their grandkids about.

The average total trip time through the tunnel was eight minutes, and 51,694 cars took the trip on that first day. There were shouts and cheers as drivers went through.

Today the toll is $4.00, and more than one billion vehicles have used the Holland Tunnel. In 1984 it was given special status as a National Civil Engineering Landmark by the American Society of Civil Engineers, the first vehiclular tunnel to gain that recognition.

The Holland Tunnel was built to handle eight million vehicles, and it has gone far beyond that expectation. The motto posted outside the New York City entrance of the tunnel says it all: "He builded better than he knew."

Battle of the Century
· 1921 ·

The scowling "Manassa Mauler," Jack Dempsey, and the handsome Frenchman known as "The Pride of Paris," Georges Carpentier, were about to engage in the biggest boxing match in fighting history. This was the match that would make boxing a legitimate sport, and it was promoted by the Don King of the day, Tex Rickard, who was so skilled at publicity it was said that "he could get a Scotsman to spend his life savings to see a marble match."

It was a match made in promoter's heaven, a good versus evil clash. In one corner was the burly, black-haired William Harrison Dempsey, known as Jack since the beginning of his fighting career, who was at the peak of his profession. He was a rugged, carefree, twenty-six-year-old American with Irish, Scottish, and Indian blood flowing through his veins. Raised on a farm until age seven in Manassa, Colorado, he later moved to Salt Lake City with his parents and seven siblings and worked as a farmer and miner. He had engaged in his first bout at the age of nineteen for the whopping sum of $23. Pound for pound, Dempsey was one of the forty hardest punchers in boxing history and had twenty-six first-round knockouts in his career. He came to the ring unshaven to scare his opponents but was very cordial with the press. As the present heavyweight champion, his fighting skills were respected, but his morals were not, for Jack Dempsey was a draft dodger.

In the other corner was the handsome twenty-seven-year-old blond Georges Carpentier, born in Lens, France, who had engaged in eighty-five bouts and had been fighting for almost fifteen years, three times as long as Dempsey. Carpentier started out as a brewery clerk, developed into a performer with a French troupe of singers, dancers, and gymnasts, and then graduated into the boxing ring at the tender age of thirteen. At age fourteen, he made his professional debut, one of the youngest of all time. With a keen intellect and highly developed speed and agility, he managed to hold every title in French boxing, from flyweight to heavyweight, and scored knockouts in every one! He even refereed a heavyweight title fight in 1913 (Johnson vs. Spoul) long before he knew he'd ever be in one against Dempsey. On top of all this, Carpentier was a war hero, a lieutenant in the French Air Force in World War I, and had been awarded the Croix de Guerre and Medaille Militaire.

Everyone wanted to see these two duke it out, especially promoter Tex Rickard. So the contract was signed and the battle was set for July 2, 1921. There was only one problem: There was no place to hold the event.

In 1921, even though sheriffs were no longer arresting the participants in the ring, many people were still morally disgusted by boxing and didn't want matches held in their town. They just couldn't understand a sport that would promote two grown men beating each other's brains out. Boxing was a lot more brutal back then, with a bout usually being stopped only when the ring floor was too slippery to continue the fight because of all the blood.

Women wouldn't dream of going to such a horrendous event, and clergymen thought it should be banned. Nonetheless, prizefighting had been made legal in New York, the place where the two biggest and most desirable arenas were: Madison Square Garden and the Polo Grounds. Rickard had planned to hold the event at Madison Square Garden, especially since he had signed a ten-year lease there the previous year with the financial backing of circus promoter John Ringling and was operating the arena. But New York Governor Nathan Miller was morally against professional boxing and refused to let the event be held in the state.

Good ol' Tex would not let his plans be foiled. He put out the word, and soon cities starting offering their sites. Rickard wanted to hold the event as close to New York City as possible, since it was considered the publicity capital of the world.

In April of 1921 New Jersey's Governor Edwards came to the rescue and offered New Jersey as the host state, narrowing the sites to Newark, Atlantic City, and Jersey City. Rickard jumped at the offer. The winning bid came from boxing enthusiast Frank Hague, mayor of Jersey City, whose political pull probably had a lot to do with it.

The site now was set, but there was another minor problem. With only ninety days left to show time, there was no Jersey City arena big enough to hold the anticipated crowd of thousands. Rickard, the eternal optimist, decided to build one. He leased a plot of land for six months and immediately sent hundreds of workers there to feverishly start building an oval-shaped arena. The original plans called for 50,000 seats. But as ticket sales kept pouring in, the pinewood arena was increased to 70,000 seats and then 90,000!

Those who purchased the $50 ringside seats had nothing to worry about. But those poor chaps in the $5.50 general admission nosebleed seats were buying a ticket not only for a world-class fight but an amusement ride as well. The shaky seats on top vibrated when people lower in the arena stomped or stood up. It was like "the wave," only this time it wasn't just people moving, it was also all the seats! When the construction was finished, it was said that from an ariel view, the arena looked like a giant sugar cube covered with thousands of flies.

The media followed every move the two fighters made in the weeks before the bout, and Rickard used all of this to his advantage. He knew he couldn't build a bigger arena, but he could surely have a bigger audience. So when Julius Hopp, the manager of Madison Square Garden, approached Rickard and his partner, Ringling, with the idea to broadcast the Dempsey-Carpentier fight, they were enthusiastic.

According to *Wireless Age* magazine, "All Hopp had to do was find a radio transmitter and an audience. At the time the *only* people who had transmitters and receivers were government, amateur radio operators, and commercial firms. Hopp approached many people and was told that the 'scheme was impractical.'" But Hopp thought the fight should be broadcast, and he persevered. He got engineer J. Owen Smith and Wireless Press vice president Andrew White interested.

After a long series of meetings and events, and some crafty engineering to get around "guidelines" for transmission, a telephone line was installed from ringside to a nearby telephone so the fight could be recorded and reports read over the air by White. As the *New York Times* reported, "It was the first time in the history of boxing matches that wireless telephony had been used to broadcast the details of a bout. Three ordinary phones were placed ringside. These were used to send the news to the big wireless telephone station in Hoboken, where the largest aerials in commercial use relayed the details to eighty points within a radius of 120,000 square miles. It was said that at least 500,000 people received the news of the fight in this manner."

Broadcast enthusiasm didn't stop there. One very inventive guy, Harold Warren, paraded a "roller chair" in Asbury Park that was equipped with a radio receiver so people could listen to the fight broadcast on the boardwalk.

While all this publicity was going on, the two fighters were training in very different ways. Carpentier set up camp in a high-class section of Manhasset, Long Island. The press and public were barred from his workouts.

Dempsey, however, trained in Atlantic City, and when not in the ring, he talked to anyone who was around. He was often seen running along the shore, engaged in rigorous training.

With the fight date drawing near, the Clergymen Community Club of New Jersey, outraged at the fascination with this immoral sport, sent a letter demanding that Mayor Hague cancel the fight. They warned it would corrupt the standards of the city. But the mayor wanted to see the fight himself, and even if he hadn't wanted to, it had already taken on a life of its own, and he couldn't stop it.

Finally it was fight day, July 2, 1921. Carpentier got up at half past six, ate a light breakfast at seven, and a took a leisurely walk around his training grounds at eight. He did not look like a man who was about to step into the ring with one of the greatest fighters of his time. Reporters who were hanging around noted how calm he seemed. He was even singing "Hail, Hail the Gang's All Here." He planned to leave at a quarter to eleven to arrive at the arena by two.

Dempsey, meanwhile, read the morning paper to see what had been written about the fight.

The arena gates opened at nine o'clock in the morning, and throngs of people flooded in. It seemed everyone was there. There was a record number of women and notables from oil magnates and bankers to legislators, politicians, and military men (some were wounded soldiers who had been given free tickets by Rickard). J. P. Morgan, Henry Ford, John D. Rockefeller, Douglas Fairbanks, George M. Cohan, and Al Jolson were there. Spectators continued to pile in until all 91,163 seats were filled. This would be the biggest crowd to ever see a prizefight!

Rickard ran into Dempsey's dressing room and yelled, "Jack! Jack! You've never seen anything like it. We got a million dollars in already, and they're still coming! And the people, Jack! I never seen anything like the people we got at this fight. High-class society folk—you name 'em, they're here. And dames! I mean classy dames, thousands of them!"

Four Secret Service men were on hand, watching receipts

to make sure the government got its share and also to prevent illegal filming from the roof of a nearby building. Herbert Gilson, attorney for the International Reform Bureau, was also there to make sure no laws were broken.

Jersey City was well prepared and had taken precautions to make sure everything went off without a hitch. The local fire department had previously doused the wooden seats with water to prevent them from easily catching on fire by a careless toss of a cigar. All flammables had to be left outside the arena, and 400 firemen were standing alert. Three thousand police officers and detectives were there to handle the crowds, scalpers, and pickpockets. There was even an emergency hospital set up outside the arena just in case someone got trampled.

At 2:56 P.M., while the ring was crowded with photographers, Carpentier suddenly appeared, wrapped in his gray dressing gown. The crowd cheered and waved hats as he clasped his hands and shook them at the audience. With the crowd still cheering, he went to his corner and talked with his manager as the band played "Marseillaise."

At exactly 3:00 P.M. the champ, Dempsey, climbed into the ring dressed in a maroon sweater and white trunks with a red, white, and blue ribbon attached to them. His entrance brought a loud cheer as well. He nodded and smiled at the crowd. As he turned away, his trademark scowl appeared on his unshaven face. He was ready to get down to business.

The two men looked at each other. Then, as if on cue, the gray-eyed, blonde, classy challenger, weighing in at 172 pounds, and the dark-haired, scowling fighter, weighing in at 188 pounds, walked to the center of the ring, shook hands, and then retreated to their corners to get taped.

When all the preliminaries were finished at 3:16 P.M., the first bell rang. The Fight of the Century had begun and both men grinned.

ROUND ONE: To the surprise of the experts, Carpentier rushed in with a fierce eagerness and aimed at Dempsey's head. He landed lightly with a left, missing a long right swing that came with startling speed and then coming into a clinch where he caught Dempsey's chin. The lighter Frenchman was agile and OK as long as he stayed out of Dempsey's close range. But Dempsey was quick, too, and landed a jolting blow on the body of the Frenchman. The champion's heavy arm then swung over Carpentier's shoulder, and his right hand found Carpentier's head five times in quick sucession. Carpentier could not stop nor pin down the champion's colossal arms. Dempsey bloodied the challengers nose. The first round went to Dempsey.

ROUND TWO: Crouching low, Dempsey forced Carpentier around the ring. Suddenly Carpentier leaped in with a left jab and followed with a right high on Dempsey's head. Dempsey pounded his rival's stomach. Then Carpentier shot a right to Dempsey's jaw with such force that it sprained his wrist and broke his thumb. The powerful blow made its mark. It dazed the champ. He staggered. The crowd was in a frenzy. They quickly encouraged Carpentier to go in for the kill—they wanted him to win. Over anxiously, Carpentier went in again and missed and ended up in a clinch. Dempsey grazed Carpentier's face with a right, which raised blood under his left eye. Carpentier's round.

ROUND THREE: With a rough massage and ice-cold water, the champ come back to his senses. The titleholder was once again on the offense, Carpentier on the defense. Carpentier was now retreating. He landed a right to Dempsey's jaw at long range. In a clinch, Dempsey pounded his rival severely about the stomach, then shifted his attack by clubbing his right to the back of Carpentier's neck in his famous "rabbit punch." A final right under the heart made Carpentier's knees give way.

Carpentier was in distress. The bell came to his rescue. Dempsey's round.

ROUND FOUR: The one-minute intermission between the rounds gave Carpentier the needed time to revive himself. He was eager to enter the ring again. Dempsey seemed to have had enough. He pounded Carpentier with powerful blows to the midsection. The challenger winced. Then quick as bolt of lightning, Dempsey landed a blow flush to the challenger's jaw. Carpentier crumpled to the floor, face down. The crowd was hushed. Their idol was on the verge of defeat. It didn't matter that Dempsey was the American, they wanted Carpentier to win. The referee began the count. As he was about to complete the ten-second count, Carpentier sprang to his feet. The crowd went wild. Dempsey immediately went in for the kill. He was smiling grimly now, confident of his victory. His mighty right hand was poised for the final blow. The champion brushed aside feeble attempts by Carpentier. Then Dempsey delivered a blow to the heart. Carpentier quivered, and a right to the jaw brought him once again to the mat. The count began again. At eight, Carpentier tried but could not get up. Nine . . . Ten . . . It was over.

At one minute and sixteen seconds into the fourth round, the champ had defended his title. Dempsey walked over to Carpentier and assisted him, showing his sportsmanship to the huge crowd. Dempsey's first thought after the fight was to telegram his mother: "Dear Mother: Won in the fourth round. Received your wire. Will be home soon as possible. Love and kisses. Jack."

After the fight the two men had only great things to say about each other. "You've got to hand it to Carpentier, he was surely game," said Dempsey. Carpentier said of Dempsey, "Jack's punch is like the kick of a mule. Everything was as fair as it could be. America should be proud of Dempsey. He is a great champion."

In the end everyone was a winner. Jersey City had the biggest prizefight there ever had been up to that time. Tex Rickard was the first boxing promoter to bring in over a million dollars. Dempsey got $300,000 (and was not arrested after the fight for assault on Carpentier, as the attorney for the International Reform Bureau demanded), Carpentier got $200,000, and the U.S. government got a total of $1,000,000 in taxes from all sources.

And on that same day, while papers all over the world were printing pages and pages about the fight, America won twice. President Warren G. Harding signed a treaty formally ending World War I, although you'd never know it; this news only received one small column in the paper, "Harding Ends War." Maybe Harding should have hired Tex Rickard as his publicist. Either way, it was a great day for New Jersey and the world.

Through the Eyes of a Dog

· 1929 ·

"Not blindness, but the attitude of the seeing to the
blind is the hardest burden to bear."

—Helen Keller

When Dorothy Harrison Eustis wrote an article for the
November 5, 1927, edition of the *Saturday Evening Post*, she
had no idea of the chain of events she would set off. The article would lead to the establishment of America's first guide dog
school, located in the quaint upscale city of Morristown.

Dorothy was a Philadelphia native who had moved to
Switzerland upon her second marriage. There she operated a
kennel called Fortune Fields with the mission to breed into
German shepherds the traits she knew they were capable of:
alertness, stamina, and responsibility. She and Jack Humphrey,
a superb animal trainer with knowledge of genetics, also hoped
to breed a work ethic into the dogs.

The desire to please a human master seems to be uniquely
canine. Other animals will work for food, but dogs will work
simply because they know it will please their masters. People
who visited Dorothy's kennel were amazed at the work ethic,
talent, and intelligence of the dogs they found there. The

Saturday Evening Post asked Dorothy to write an article about her work, but instead of writing about her own facility, she decided to focus on a school located in Potsdam, Germany, where German shepherds were being trained to work as guide dogs for blinded World War I veterans. The article, entitled "The Seeing Eye," began:

> To everyone, I think there is always something particularly pathetic about a blind man. Shorn of his strength and his independence, he is prey to all the sensitiveness of his position, and he is at the mercy of all with whom he comes into contact. . . . In darkness and uncertainty he must start over again, wholly dependent on outside help for every move. His other senses may rally to his aid, but they cannot replace his eyesight. To man's never failing friend has been accorded this special privilege. Gentlemen, I give you the German Shepherd dog!

Dorothy didn't expect much of a response to her article. After all, guide dogs for the blind were nothing new. Throughout history there have been depictions of blind people being led by dogs. One dating back to 100 B.C. shows a blind Germanic king with a guide dog. But the unexpected happened. Hundreds of letters from America poured in. Blind people had heard about the article and wanted to know more. But Dorothy and Jack were breeders, not trainers. How could they help?

One letter particularly affected Dorothy. It was from a nineteen-year-old named Morris Frank. This young man from Nashville had been blinded by a tree limb while riding a horse at age sixteen. Morris wrote, "If you would give me the address of this school in Germany, or of any trainer in this country who might have anything similar as I should like very much to forward this work in this country. . . . Thousands of blind like me abhor being dependent on others. Help me and I will help them." His letter rambled on almost without punctuation, but Dorothy immediately felt she wanted to help the young man.

Dorothy and Morris began to correspond. Morris told her he was perfectly willing to pay her to train a dog and bring it to the United States. Dorothy suggested that Morris come to Switzerland instead and work with a dog that he could then take back to the States. Morris jumped at the chance. "Mrs. Eustis, to get my independence back, I'd go to hell."

Dorothy planned to purchase a trained dog from Potsdam and then have Jack briefly work with the dog before passing him on to Morris, but Potsdam refused to sell her a guide dog. So they decided this one time that Jack would train his own dog from Fortune Fields.

Jack believed that guide dogs need to be educated, not trained. He taught Morris and his dog, Buddy, to work together as an inseparable team based on love and friendship rather than obedience. Jack instilled in Morris a philosophy that Morris always remembered and later made the motto of his school: "A blind person must help himself so that the school can help him. Independence and dignity are key."

While working with Buddy, Morris went through a series of emotions: uncertainty, anxiety, anger, panic, love, confidence, and exhilaration. Wearing silent rubber-soled shoes, Jack followed the pair as they walked together. He purposely stepped on Buddy's paw, bumped into Morris, and let them make mistakes so they would learn to deal with all types of situations. At one point, Jack let them go to the edge of a lake and then told Morris to feel around with his cane. Jack laughed, "Let that teach you never to step off the curb ahead of your dog."

The first time Buddy and Morris went solo, Buddy (with Morris's instructions) navigated Morris to the barbershop. It was the first time in four years that he had been able to go somewhere without a human companion. He was thrilled and exclaimed, "By God, I'm free."

Morris and Buddy traveled to America and did several press conferences. Dorothy, Morris, and Buddy went on a cross-country tour of schools and corporations, promoting the benefits of guide dogs. It took a lot of legwork and determination to get the blind organizations to trust the dogs and to get the dogs accepted in public places, but eventually they won out. Morris was even received in the White House by President Herbert Hoover. Morris never gave up. He had a dream, and he made it a reality. He said, "This work shall not fail, and by the God that made me, I shall leave no stone unturned until The Seeing Eye is in a firm running basis."

Morris opened his first office in Nashville, Tennessee, in February 1929 with seventeen students. As the business grew, it needed a permanent location with a cooler climate to accommodate the intense physical training needed. He chose Morristown as the site for the school.

On November 10, 1931, The Seeing Eye, named after Dorothy's article, was opened. Dorothy and subsequent charitable donations financed it, but Morris ran it. The school covered fifty acres on Whippany Road. Several pretrained dogs that had been raised in volunteer homes by 4-H Club members were ready to be matched up with students.

The night before they were to close on the property and open the school, one more test of fate happened. The local zoning board wanted to ban the property from being used as a guide school. A bold step was made, and the students who had been waiting in a nearby hotel were moved in without heat, light, telephones, or water. There were no supplies, the kitchen was bare, and the furniture was just piled up. But the crew managed it. They moved heaven, earth, and themselves into the house. They had the first supper there Tuesday night, fourteen at the table. Morris declared, "It is the realization of our dream to be at the head of the table with eight blind people and eight bright-eyed dogs under the table."

The Seeing Eye school had been saved, and the threat of preventing it from opening nullified.

On the first day of operation, the eight students were awakened to begin their training. The Seeing Eye was about to teach them to become independent and to teach Morristown about the blind.

They were driven into town in the darkness of early morning. As the sun rose, Morristown residents gathered to watch the students take their first practice walk with their dogs and instructors. During the first run the instructor held one end of the dog harness while the student held the U-shaped handle on the other end and followed. The instructor demonstrated how to give essential commands, drop the harness, tug on the leash, and verbally reprimand the dog if necessary. While teaching, the instructors were also assessing each student's strength, agility, coordination, and walking speed so that they could be matched with a permanent dog. The dog's job was to see obstacles and avoid them; the person's job was to command and direct the dog to the desired location along the desired route.

Having a new guide dog school nearby required some adaption for Morristown citizens. When a dog got too close to a moving car, an instructor would slap the fender of the car and utter the worst word in the guide dog vocabulary, "Pfui." The word is spoken with venom, letting the dog know something is wrong. Some Morristown residents weren't happy about having their cars slapped.

Pedestrians also had to watch out, lest they be bumped or stepped on by inexperienced students working with their dogs. Even bank customers had to be wary. The bank had the only revolving door in town, and the owners gave the school permission to use the door for practice. Unfortunately, during one training session a dog suffered a diarrhea attack, leaving the instructor frantically trying to clean up the mess as customers tried to get into the bank.

Some residents claimed it was cruel to have the dogs in harnesses, but the U-shaped apparatus had been specially chosen to allow the blind to feel the movements of the dog but cause no pain to the animal. A few Morristown residents tried to help the blind students, not realizing that it had dire effects on their training. Grabbing a blind person's arm or dog is like grabbing the steering wheel from someone driving. One student remembered, "I was helped back and forth across the same street three times by well-meaning people."

In the end, everyone got used to working together.

When that first group of students finally went solo, all involved were thrilled. The blind experienced a renewed feeling of independence. The instructors' voices played in their heads as they walked the streets: "Don't grip the harness too tight!" "She's trying to lead you—follow!" "Every service of the dog must be rewarded with 'Atta good girl' spoken in a tone of rapture."

After twenty-seven days of training, The Seeing Eye's first Morristown class graduated. Within about six months, each duo was working well together, able to blend effortlessly into a crowd.

As of 2002, The Seeing Eye has matched nearly 13,000 dogs with men and women from across the United States and Canada, earning it a place in the *Guinness Book of World Records*.

Everyone recognizes how special these dogs are. In some instances, the dogs have saved lives, instinctively knowing to disobey a command of "Forward" if there appeared to be danger. Over the years the school has gained much recognition. The Walt Disney Company made a three-part television series called *Atta Girl, Kelly*, and several books have been written about the school, including one it considers its bible, *Love in the Lead*.

Today the school is housed in a new facility, complete with its own revolving door and modern medical technology that can detect genetic problems in puppies. Besides German shepherds, the school also trains Labradors and golden retrievers. In keeping with Dorothy, Jack, and Morris's philosophy, they work "with" blind people rather than "for" them. The school has supplied dogs free of charge to veterans and maintains the policy that no one shall be turned down due to lack of money. The Seeing Eye thrives solely on contributions, bequests, and income from endowments and trusts.

Lindbergh Baby Kidnapped
· 1932 ·

Betty Gow raced down the hallway of the luxurious retreat on Sourland Mountain shouting, "Mrs. Lindbergh, have you got the baby?" Anne Lindbergh replied, "No." The nursemaid tore down the steps, with Anne at her heels, and ran into the library where Charles Lindbergh was reading, "Colonel, have YOU got the baby?," Betty panted. "Isn't he in the crib?," Lindbergh replied. And at that moment they knew—Chas was gone.

They were known as "the most romantic and adventurous couple of all time." Colonel Charles A. Lindbergh had become a household name as the first man to fly across the Atlantic nonstop in his plane, the *Spirit of St. Louis,* in May of 1927, covering 3,600 miles from Long Island to Paris. On his second long-distance solo flight from New York to Mexico City, he met his future wife, Anne Morrow, daughter of a U.S. ambassador, and they fell in love. Charles had met his match, and soon the two were flying together and pioneering many of today's modern airplane routes. The newspapers and the world followed their adventures.

This couple had everything—fame, money, happiness, and their beautiful blonde curly-haired son, Chas. Because of their fame, the idea that someone might kidnap their child lingered in the minds of the Lindberghs, so they took the necessary precautions. They never revealed to newspapers the room in which their adorable son slept in their Hopewell, New Jersey, home. But an evil fate intervened.

On March 1, 1932, as Charles was reading in his library, he heard an odd sharp cracking sound. He paused for a moment, but then there was silence, so he went back to reading his book. Since it was a slightly cold night the nurse decided to turn up the electric heater in the nursery. Feeling maternal, she tiptoed over to Chas's crib in the darkened room. She paused at his crib and did not hear breathing. Then she reached her hand down and felt the cold emptiness. Twenty-month-old Chas was not there. Betty ran to his parents with screams and questions. When Charles saw the empty crib, he remembered the cracking sound he had heard earlier that night. They later found out that the sound was that of a ladder step being broken as the kidnapper was getting away. The ladder now rested outside against Chas's bedroom window wall.

Charles immediately, in keeping with his way of calmness in crisis, instructed his wife to "get the butler to call the police and don't touch anything." He then walked over to the closet where he kept his Springfield rifle and went outside to look for any signs of life. The only sound was the wind whistling through the barren tree branches. The lonely night engulfed him. He went inside to console Anne and wait for the police to arrive.

The police station sent out an all points bulletin along the entire eastern coast of the United States. The message read "Lindbergh Baby kidnapped from his home near Hopewell, New Jersey. Stop and search all cars."

The police found very few clues: barely detectable footprints, a chisel, and a makeshift ladder in three parts with one step broken in the top section. The final clue was a ransom note found on the window sill of the nursery. It was filled with misspellings and an unusual signature of two interlocking circles, one red and one blue. Each circle had a hole in the center. The way the circles were drawn led the detectives to believe the kidnapper was German. The signature was kept secret by the police in order to keep anyone from trying to forge it and throw the investigation off. The note asked the Lindberghs to "have $50,000 dollars redy. . . . After 2–4 days we will inform you were to deliver the mony. . . . The child is in gut care. Instruction for letters are signature."

Two hundred thousand letters of sympathy arrived for the Lindberghs. The police, FBI, and Secret Service, along with reporters, photographers, and America's top private detectives, were on the case. Even incarcerated mobster Al Capone promised to recover baby Lindbergh if he was granted his freedom in return.

America sympathized with the pain of the Lindberghs, whose only hope was the note that said their baby was "in gut care." Emotionally tortured, Mrs. Lindbergh made a tearful plea to take care of her baby that was broadcast throughout the United States, Canada, and Mexico. The kidnapper sent her a note assuring her that Chas was okay.

A week later, on March 8, Dr. John Condon, a teacher and lecturer from the Bronx, sent a heartfelt letter to the *Bronx Home News* addressed to the kidnapper, asking him to return the baby. "For the sake of his own mother, that he may offer restitution for his crime, I offer all that I could scrape together, 1,000 dollars of my own money, so that a loving mother may again have her darling child, so that people will know that the greatest criminal in the world has a bright spot in his heart. . . . I write of my own free will, that no testimony of mine or coming from me will be used against him, this is an appeal for the sake of humanity."

The kidnapper responded in a letter with the red and blue circles as his mark. A nighttime rendezvous was set up for March 12 in Woodlawn Cemetery. Dr. Condon went with a friend, Al Reich, a former heavyweight boxer, to meet the kidnapper. The kidnapper identified himself as "John" and let the doctor see his face for future meetings. He identified baby pins belonging to Chas, and Dr. Condon was convinced he was the real kidnapper.

Correspondence began between the doctor and "John." The kidnapper asked for $70,000 and later $100,000 if the money wasn't paid by April 8. He told Dr. Condon the baby was safe and alive and gave him the boy's pajamas as proof he was the real kidnapper.

At St. Raymond's Cemetery on the night of April 2, Dr. Condon and Colonel Lindbergh went to meet the kidnapper with $70,000. Unknown to either of them, the U.S. Treasury had listed the serial numbers of every single bill.

Lindbergh sat in the car, anxiously waiting to be reunited with his child, while Dr. Condon went into the woods to talk to the kidnapper. The kidnapper refused to hand the baby over before he got the money, saying he wanted eight hours to make his getaway, then the whereabouts of Chas would be revealed. In one last desperate attempt, to get the kidnapper to sympathize and hand over the baby, Dr. Condon told the kidnapper that Lindbergh was only able to raise $50,000. He convinced the kidnapper to take the $50,000 instead.

The next day they received instructions on where to find Chas: "The boy is on the boad Nelly. It is a small boad 28 feet long. Two persons are on the boad. They are innocent. You will find the boad between Horseneck Beach and Gay Head, near Elizabeth Island."

Colonel Lindbergh, Dr. Condon, and a friend flew to the location of the boat off the coast of Massachusetts. No one had ever heard of the *Nelly*. The boat did not exist. It was then that Lindbergh knew he'd never see his son again.

Lindbergh released all the details in a desperate effort to catch the kidnapper. By May 12 all hope was gone. Then William Allen, a truck driver, happened to be walking in the woods near the Lindbergh home, and came across a shallow grave containing the body of a decomposed infant with golden hair and a homemade shirt. It turned out that Chas had been killed the night of the kidnapping by a severe blow to his head. Anne Lindbergh, numb, had to identify her baby's body.

The world now cried for vengeance. The couple that had changed the world had had their most prized possession snatched away from them. Everyone wanted answers.

Nurse Betty Gow became a suspect, but charges against her were dismissed. Violet Sharpe, the Lindbergh maid, committed suicide when she was accused. Slowly answers began to be revealed. Police suspected the kidnapper lived in the Bronx because of his quick reply to Dr. Condon's letter. Arthur Koehler, a U.S. Forestry Service expert, was able to trace the ladder's lumber to the forest it had grown in, to the mill it was processed in, to the store that had sold it to the kidnapper. But the store had no records that proved helpful.

Pure luck intervened. On May 1, 1934, President Franklin Roosevelt abandoned the gold standard. At the time, the United States used both regular money as we know it and gold certificates. One September day at ten in the morning, a man used a gold certificate to buy five gallons of gas. The gas station attendant got suspicious since he hadn't seen a gold certificate in a while and took down the license plate number. At the bank, the teller traced the certificate and found it had one of the serial numbers of the Lindbergh ransom money. The license plate number was traced to an illegal German immigrant, Bruno Richard Hauptmann.

On September 19, 1934, Hauptmann was arrested and found with another marked bill in his pocket. In the garage of his house, in a shellac can under some old rags, they found $11,930 in gold certificates. As they took the garage apart, they found more and more of the ransom money.

On January 2, 1935, Hauptmann's trial began. To the end, even with all the evidence against him, Hauptmann pleaded his innocence. To this day no one knows if he deliberately killed the baby or if Chas fell to his death when the ladder step broke. Hauptmann was unanimously convicted of the murder of the Lindbergh baby and sentenced to death.

What's *Behind* This Invention?

· 1933 ·

It is often said that necessity is the mother of invention, but who would have thought that the large behind of a woman would create a fad that would start in New Jersey and then catch on around the country? That fad was the drive-in movie theater, and that large behind belonged to the mother of Richard M. Hollingshead, Jr. His mother was a large woman. She was so large that she couldn't fit comfortably into the seats at the local movie theater in Camden County. Jokingly she commented to her son that it would nice if she could just watch a movie from the plush seat of her car. That comment got Richard thinking.

In the 1930s Richard was a sales manager at his dad's Whiz Auto Products store. The thought of making his mom happy and inventing something that would combine two of his hobbies—cars and movies—was an opportunity he couldn't pass up.

He began experimenting in his own driveway at 212 Thomas Avenue in Camden. The first thing he did was mount a 1928 Kodak projector onto the hood of his car. Then he nailed a giant screen to some trees that were on his property. To top it off, he placed a radio behind the screen for sound. Now he had the three components he needed: comfort, picture, and sound. With that as a starting point, he began a series of vigorous tests to see how he could get the best results. As he began testing, his excitement grew and thoughts started racing in his head. Why just do it for mom? Others may have this problem, too. Why not do it for everyone? He now thought on a larger scale.

Richard began with the sound. He wanted to make sure it could be heard in all types of weather. He used his sprinkler to simulate rain, then would determine how loud or close the radio had to be without getting drowned out.

The next thing he had to figure out was the logistics. He needed to arrange the cars in such a way that all the people inside them would be able to see the movie. He lined up cars in his driveway and got in and out of each one to make sure the people inside would have a good view. At this point, his neighbors all thought he had gone nuts, running in and out of the cars like a madman. Richard didn't care. He was on a mission. He realized after several episodes of musical chairs with the cars that if he spaced them at various distances and placed blocks or makeshift ramps under the front wheels of cars that were far away, he changed their line of vision and allowed them to face the screen unobstructed. He felt he'd created the perfect parking arrangement.

The last element was the screen. He kept making it bigger and bigger until he felt it could comfortably accommodate several dozen cars.

After having worked out the kinks in his driveway, he decided to put some money behind his idea. With $30,000 in investment capital and a U.S. patent (#1-909-537) on June 7, 1933, Richard opened the world's first drive-in movie theater on Crescent Boulevard in Camden. His mom was pleased—and comfortable.

He used the parking lot of his dad's automotive parts store on what is now Admiral Wilson Boulevard (formerly Bridge Boulevard), near the border of Camden and Pennsauken, as the theater area. It was set up in a fan-shaped fashion, complete with tiered parking and inclined ramps. For the movie itself, he used a 16-millimeter projector. For the screen, his dad's store came into use once again. The white back wall of the store became a 30-by-40-foot screen for projection. And finally for sound, Richard cut a deal with RCA Victor to provide three large speakers mounted next to the screen. It wasn't the greatest setup for the cars in the rear or for the neighbors, but no one really seemed too upset.

His first night was a big success. More than 400 cars lined up in eight rows to watch and experience the family-oriented movie shown at the world's first "automobile movie theater." The price of admission was 25 cents for the car and 25 cents per person.

Richard Hollingshead had a hit on his hands. He and his cousin decided to capitalize on it and create a drive-in movie franchise throughout the United States called Park-In Theatres Inc. They would show family movies, charging $1.00 per family or 75 cents for two people.

Park-in Theatres sprung up around the country. People loved the fact that they could see a movie without getting dressed up; some even brought their kids in their pajamas. Patrons could get out of their cars if they wanted to, to get food, wash their cars, or play shuffleboard and even miniature golf, since many of the franchise owners offered these services, all geared toward making more money.

Traditional movie houses started to get nervous—they recognized the threat that these drive-in movies were creating. They made it difficult for the park-ins to get first-run features in a timely manner and would also give them shorter edited versions of films. Still, people came.

As the business grew, Richard worked on perfecting it. He enhanced the sound quality by placing individual speakers on each car. In 1949 his patent was overturned. Now having free rein, with no patent to worry about, everyone went park-in crazy.

By the 1950s the term "drive-in movie theater" had been coined. There were nearly 4,000 drive-in theaters nationwide, with the largest in Copiague, New York, consisting of a twenty-eight-acre lot capable of holding 2,500 cars, and an additional indoor seating area capable of holding 1,200 people, a playground, a full-service restaurant, and a shuttle train to take customers all around the All-Weather Drive-In.

The two smallest drive-ins were in Bamberg, South Carolina, with each only able to accommodate fifty cars. One New Jersey drive-in collected a defense tax on its admission to help the military during World War II. The most unusual drive-in was also a *fly-in*—Ed Brown's Drive-In and Fly-In, located in Asbury Park. In this unique twist, an airfield capable of holding twenty-five planes was placed next to the drive-in, and planes would taxi to the last row of the theater. When the movie was over, a tow for the planes was provided to get them back to the airfield so they could be free to fly up into the night sky.

The drive-in's success tailed off in the 1970s when the rising cost of real estate made it illogical to keep the land just for the theaters and when cable television and video rental outlets allowed people to see movies even more comfortably from their own homes.

Today there are about 500 active drive-in movie theaters around the country. None, however, are left in New Jersey, the birthplace of these theaters. When they bulldozed the last lot they probably took out the spirit. But by then the good deed was done by one New Jersey son. Thank goodness Hollingshead's mother wasn't a vegetarian or we may never have had the experience.

Lighter Than Air Travel Ends with a Big Bang

· 1937 ·

In March of 1936 the brand-new silver 804-foot-long rigid airship, the *Hindenburg*, standing 135 feet tall, or 16 stories high, with two swastikas on its tail fins, was "walked" out like a big balloon on ropes from a hangar in Friedrichshafen, Germany.

Since airships could be, and often were, easily damaged by clumsy ground crews or even strong winds, the Germans wanted to take extra care. This was the *Hindenburg*'s maiden voyage—a three-day propaganda flight to distribute leaflets over Germany.

Suddenly a crosswind of 18 miles per hour lifted the ship and threw its tail to the ground, damaging it. Dr. Hugo Eckener—a popular German hero and associate of the late Count Ferdinand von Zeppelin (aka the "Crazy Count"), the inventor of the first rigid airship and cofounder of DELAG, the first passenger airline—had mixed emotions. As the successful director of the Luftschiffbau Zeppelin Company, Eckener was strongly against the zeppelin (airship) being used as a symbol of Nazi power. He'd made his opinions known and refused to be present at this event. His anti-Nazi sentiments may have played a big factor in the later destruction of the *Hindenburg* in New Jersey on that fateful day, May 6, 1937, when the world would watch it explode.

But for now, on this March day, despite his opposition, the tail of the airship was quickly repaired, and after a short weather delay, the *Hindenburg,* the pride of Germany and the Zeppelin company, took off on it's first voyage.

By May 3, 1937, the *Hindenburg* had already completed several successful and well-publicized flights. It had flown over South America, had a famous "Millionaire's Flight," had made several record-breaking flights from Germany to the United States, and had even flown over the Olympic Games in Berlin.

Despite the swastikas, the *Hindenburg* was both American and German owned. As part of an agreement at the end of World War I and the Treaty of Versailles, the Germans had to turn over all their zeppelins to the Allies as war reparations, since Germany was the only nation that had used its airships offensively, to conduct air raids that killed about 2,000 people, mostly civilians, during the war. The French claimed the Germans built the *L-72*—a zeppelin that had been built to bomb New York. The United States, interested in developing a military airship program, got a special waiver to the Treaty of Versailles that allowed the Germans to build the *Hindenburg*, a custom-made, transoceanic airship. Thus in 1923 a German-American business alliance was formed, the Goodyear-Zeppelin Corporation, a subsidiary of Goodyear Tire and Rubber, which assumed ownership of all the zeppelin patents. The Germans, largely financed by the Nazi party, built the *Hindenburg,* and the Americans built the largest airship port in the world, with spark-proof floors and explosion-proof lighting, at the Lakehurst Naval Air Station in New Jersey to accommodate it.

The *D-LZ129,* renamed the *Hindenburg,* was *the* luxury liner of the air for its time. It could make a non-stop journey across the Atlantic in a record two and a half days, faster than any other method of travel. No planes had yet been built to do that. It was the largest object ever to fly, only 78½ feet shorter than the *Titanic*. Sitting next to the *Hindenburg*, a 747 jet would look tiny.

Out of the three types of airships—rigid, semirigid, and nonrigid (like the Goodyear blimp)—the *Hindenburg* was considered a rigid because of its 804-foot-long metal skeleton, which gave the ship its cigarlike shape. Inside the skeleton were sixteen enormous gasbags, called cells, which were coated with a gelatin and latex lightweight solution. These cells held the over seven-million-cubic feet of flammable hydrogen gas that gave the *Hindenburg* its lifting power.

The *Hindenburg* was originally designed to use helium, a nonflammable gas, but at that time the American government, which controlled the world's largest supply of helium, refused to sell it to the Germans for fear they would use it for military purposes, such as inflating future zeppelins for spy missions and bombings. So the Germans used hydrogen gas instead. The advantage of this was that since hydrogen has more lifting power than helium, the *Hindenburg* was able to accommodate twenty-two passengers more than originally planned, making room for a total of thirty-six passengers.

Tickets for a ride on the *Hindenburg* were not cheap. They cost $405 apiece, the cost of a car back then. Many movie stars, counts and countesses, millionaires, and newspaper reporters would ride. But ordinary people rode, too, people ranging in age from six months to ninety-three years, and the price of the ticket to most of them was well worth the experience. The infamous flight, which began May 3, was the first flight to America of the 1937 season, and the nineteenth transatlantic trip overall. It was to be like all others, first class all the way.

The living quarters of the *Hindenburg* had two floors. On Deck A there was a huge dining room with expensive china and world-class food and wine where three meals a day plus afternoon tea were served; a pantry room where the food was brought down by a dumbwaiter; two 50-foot promenade decks where passengers could observe the floor below or look out the huge slanted observation windows from built-in seats to see the ground passing below; a lounge with a grand piano and fabric-covered walls with hand-painted artwork and a map of the world showing the routes of history's most famous explorers and their ships; a reading and writing room with walls covered with the hand-painted history of postal delivery; and twenty-five passenger cabins equipped with bunkbeds and hot and cold running water.

On Deck B was the officers' mess, the kitchen, the crew's mess, a changing room, the world's first airborne shower, toilets, urinals, the chief steward's cabin, a bar, and a smoking room. Yes, believe it or not, on this highly flammable ship there was a smoking room with a single cigarette lighter chained to the wall. To get to this room, passengers had to pass through a special airtight lock. The room was pressurized to prevent any stray hydrogen from leaking in. When passengers had had their smoke and were ready to leave, they were examined by a crew member to ensure they had no lit cigarettes, cigars, or pipes or any ashes or sparks on their clothing.

To top it off, the airship, unlike today's planes, was quiet. Passengers reported being able to hear the shouts of people below or the cries of birds while in flight. With the windows opened, there was no draft, in or out, while the ship was moving. It was luxury all the way.

Safety was the main concern. The outside of the airship was painted with dope, a liquid that makes fabric waterproof and able to stretch tightly over a ship's airframe. The silver-colored aluminum particles in the *Hindenburg*'s dope also helped to reflect the sun's heat. Inside, the duralumin—the lightweight metal used to construct the skeleton of the *Hindenburg*—was covered with a bright blue coating to make it corrosion-proof.

The crew members wore asbestos suits and felt boots whenever they went near the gasbags to prevent static electricity buildup, which could spark a fire. The crew's suits didn't even have buttons or zippers, and the ladders in the upper part of the ship were coated with rubber. The four 1,300-horsepower Daimler-Benz engines that drove the ship required no ignition (which creates an electrical spark). Instead they used crude oil that wouldn't burn, supposedly, even if a flaming match were thrown into it.

The safety precautions extended to the passengers as well. As the excited thirty-six passengers boarded in Frankfurt for the May 3 flight, they underwent a routine safety inspection. All passengers had to open their bags, which were checked for anything that might produce a spark or electrical charge. Camera flashbulbs, matches, flashlights, and cigarette lighters were all confiscated by the stewards, who told the passengers they would get their items back upon landing. The Zeppelin company prided itself on the fact that in the more than twelve years that their airships had been carrying passengers, there had never been a fire. And the *Hindenburg*, which billed itself as "the safest airship ever built," was certainly not about to be the first.

Everything appeared normal as that first flight of 1937 sailed over the ocean. As the passengers basked in luxury, the sixty-one crew members walked the narrow catwalks to do inspections on the ship, checking fuel and water levels, repairing any tears in the silver fabric that covered the frame, and checking for leaks. Since hydrogen is odorless, garlic was put into the mixture so a leak could be detected immediately. Meanwhile, the captain, Max Pruss, directed the flight from the control car, located underneath the ship. He could change altitude, release water, or make the ship heavier by releasing hydrogen from vents at the top of the craft. He could also signal the four engine cars, which were also located underneath the airship and whose only means of access was to climb outside the *Hindenburg* and down a metal ladder in rubber-soled shoes, facing an ear-popping, face-freezing wind.

On May 6 the *Hindenburg* was sighted over the Lakehurst field, as it had been many times before. But this time fierce thunderstorms prevented it from landing. To pass the time, Captain Pruss took his passengers on a scenic tour over Boston, the Jersey Shore, and New York City. Cars honked, planes tipped their wings, and the airship flew over the Empire State Building so close the passengers could see the expressions on the tourists' faces. Passengers were given interesting tidbits of information, like the fact that the Empire State Building, built in 1931, was designed to serve as a dirigible station.

At 7:00 P.M., after a twelve-hour delay and having circled the Lakehurst field several times, the *Hindenburg* came in at about 500 feet above the ground. Once he was told they were safe to land, the captain made a sharp turn and began to bring the ship to earth.

The civilian ground crew of 200 men, who were each being paid a dollar, was ready as usual to grab the ropes and pull her in. Spectators and the media were on hand to witness the massive airship's landing. At 7:23 P.M. the ropes were dropped.

Herbert Morrison, a reporter for a Chicago radio station, was at the scene and giving commentary on what he thought would be a routine landing: "Here it comes, ladies and gentlemen, and what a sight it is, a thrilling one, a marvelous sight. . . . The sun is striking the windows of the observation deck on the westward side and sparkling like glittering jewels on the background of black velvet. Passengers are looking out windows waving. The ship is standing still now. The vast motors are just holding it, just enough to keep from—"

Then it happened. Some crew members heard a sound like a gunshot. A gas cell had ignited. Then there was a concussion felt hundreds of yards—even miles—away. The first burst of flame appeared near the tail of the airship and quickly spread forward.

Morrison screamed, "It's broken into flames! It's flashing,

flashing! It's flashing terrible!!! Oh, oh, oh! . . . This is one of the worst catastrophes in the world! It's a terrible sight. . . . Oh! And the humanity and all the passengers! This is the worst thing I've ever witnessed!"

The floor dropped out from underneath the passengers. Broken china was flying everywhere. Flames exploded through the walls. Tables, chairs, and silverware were tossed everywhere. Passengers screamed in terror and shoved each other out of the way.

There was no time to warn anyone, just time to react. A wave of heat and smoke rushed in as cell by cell exploded. Flames raced down the metal catwalk. Then the *Hindenburg's* stern dropped out of the sky. The only escape for passengers was to jump out the windows. Metal crashed around them. People's hair and clothing caught on fire as they jumped. The sandy soil below was burning hot. Those who jumped had to get up while burning and run before the flaming ball crashed down on them. As they ran blindly to the edge of the landing field, flames licked at their backs.

The bow was the last part to crash to the ground. Miraculously, two-thirds of the people aboard the airship fought their way through the flaming walls of fire to safety. Had the ship fallen any slower, everyone aboard would have burned to death.

Firemen fought the scorching flames, and rescuers dragged the injured away from the inferno. They were taken to local hospitals, with rescue vehicles fighting 10 miles of roads clogged by stopped spectators.

At midnight, even though the flames were out, the embers were still so hot, they could not search for bodies. When the count was in, amazingly sixty-two of the ninety-seven people aboard had survived. The total number killed included twenty-two crew members and thirteen passengers aboard, one ground crew member, and a dog below. Ironically, a lone charred letter from the mailroom that was supposed to be delivered from Holland to Germany also survived. Everything else burned away.

The *Hindenburg* fire was not the worst airship disaster in history, but it was the first time that paying passengers were injured or killed, and it was the first major disaster witnessed by photographers, radio broadcasters, and newsreel camera operators.

Although no one knows exactly what happened, several theories were reported; some blamed pilot error or engine failure. But after the German and American governments sent in a team of investigators, three theories came to prominence.

The first theory blames it on the hydrogen. This theory says that one of the metal wires that held the gasbags in place snapped as the *Hindenburg* made the sharp turn over the airfield. The snap caused the wire to tear a hole in one of the gas cells, and the freed gas mixed with oxygen and was ignited by static electricity. However, as someone pointed out, no one had smelled garlic, which would have indicated a leak.

The second theory blames the outer covering, stating that the dope, the silver liquid paint covering the zeppelin, was made of a substance like varnish mixed with aluminum powder, which is similar to the recipe for the solid rocket fuel used in space shuttles. Those who believe this theory think the thunderstorm left enough of an electrical charge in the air to ignite the cover. If this theory is correct, the *Hindenburg* would have burned whether it was filled with hydrogen or not.

The last theory blames sabotage. The *Hindenburg*'s captain, Max Pruss, and the Zeppelin company director, Hugo Eckener, both believed that the airship was destroyed deliberately due to hatred of the Nazi party. It was no secret that Eckener disliked the Nazis.

Captain Pruss went on record as saying that he thought a timed incendiary device caused the fire. At least one crew member remembered seeing a sudden glow in the number four gasbag just before the fire. There was a ladder that permitted access between cells four and five, so someone could have easily planted it. Captain Pruss stated that if there was a gas leak prior to the fire, he would have known about it through the control room instruments.

Pruss believed that the device was set to go off after six o'clock when no one would be on board, but due to the twelve-hour landing delay it went off before the ship had been vacated. He had a suspicion of who might have committed such an act but never named his suspect.

Whatever the reason, the *Hindenburg* explosion convinced people that airships were not a safe means of travel. Soon after, passenger planes were developed, making flight safer and faster.

A memory of the *Hindenburg* disaster remains in Hangar One at the Naval Air Station in Lakehurst. Several officers and personnel, then and now, have reported seeing a ghostly figure in the hangar that vanishes when approached. As Alan Gross, airship historian and president of Airships Unlimited, related,

> I was a ground crew member for a blimp from 1985 through 1989. Every year we took the blimp to Lakehurst, New Jersey, for maintenance periods. The company I worked for (Airship International Ltd.) began to use Hangar One in 1986. I was assigned the midnight watch, which meant light duty but also I had to spend the night in the huge hangar by myself. I often heard murmurs and whispers but could never identify the source. As I walked through the cavernous interior, I ran into "cold spots" and felt as if I had stepped through a spider web. These, I am told, are indications of paranormal activity but I never felt afraid and would not hesitate to stay the night again.

Others have reported that during the daylight hours outside

of the hangar, they have heard the sounds of whirling engines or men shouting, "Away the lines, Christ be blessed, away the lines!," or, "She's afire!" Some say these are the sounds of the lost souls that perished that day; others say it might be ghosts of soldiers once stationed there. Either way, the hangar and the *Hindenburg* leave chills in the annals of Jersey history.

The Halloween Joke That Scared the Nation

·1938·

It was an unsettling time, with the Great Depression still strangling America and an icy Hitler talking of war. To distract themselves, the people of Grovers Mill sat huddled with their families around the radio, ready to listen to an evening of entertainment. It was October 30, 1938, a Sunday evening, one day before Halloween. Little did these people know, they were about to become part of American history.

A popular show of the day was the *Chase and Sanborn Hour,* featuring the comedy team of ventriloquist Edgar Bergen and his wisecracking dummy, Charlie McCarthy. (Yes, believe it or not, they had ventriloquism on the radio then.) The show started at seven o'clock in the evening, but as was typical of most radio shows at the time, it went over its allotted time slot of one hour. About twelve minutes after eight, Nelson Eddy came on to sing "Neapolitan Love Song." Four million people began to channel-surf until the song was over.

Poor Eddy. Apparently people weren't in the mood for crooning, because four million listeners surfed over to an in-progress program being broadcast out of a New York studio which was in progress on WABC and the Columbia Broadcasting

System's coast-to-coast network. The program had started at eight sharp. Those just tuning in had missed the opening announcement and were being bombarded with a flood of very real sounding "news bulletins" that claimed Martians were attacking New Jersey.

What they were listening to was a special Halloween production created by the twenty-three-year-old boy genius of Broadway, Orson Welles (known for his radio character, "The Shadow," who used to give the creeps to countless children). Welles had decided to produce an updated dramatization of novelist H. G. Wells's fantasy *The War of the Worlds,* as a trick instead of a treat on Halloween. However, this little trick backfired—big time.

Ever since Welles had transplanted his highly successful off-Broadway company, the Mercury Theatre, to radio, he had wanted to adapt and present a science-fiction novel. That genre was largely untouched, with the exception of Buck Rogers, by airwaves at the time. Before he could broadcast *The War of the Worlds,* Welles felt he needed to spruce up the story, modernize it, and have it take place in America to grab the audience's interest. He also wanted the show to air for Halloween. He had six days to make this all happen—it was a task that normally took several weeks.

Welles worked at a record pace, his fingers flying furiously on the typewriter. But he did not work alone. He had his actors, the Mercury Players, and a team of writers giving input.

The identity of the final author of the script has been a matter of controversy for years. Although Welles took credit for the production, a young playwright by the name of Howard Koch has been credited with doing much of the scribe work on the revisions. Koch, wanting to please Welles on his first assignment, bought a map at a New Jersey gas station and later that night closed his eyes and blindly stabbed a pencil down to select a real town in which this fictional event was to occur.

The pencil point landed on the sleepy town of Grovers Mill, just 8 miles east of Trenton.

Had listeners tuned in at the beginning of the broadcast, they would have known that what they were about to hear was purely fiction. They would have heard this announcement: "The Columbia Broadcasting System and its affiliated stations present Orson Welles and the Mercury Theatre on the air in *The War of the Worlds* by H. G. Wells." They then would have heard Welles himself set the scene by quoting from the Wells novel (with the 1930s updates): "We now know that in the early years of the twentieth century this world was being watched closely by intelligence greater than man, yet as mortal as his own. . . ." Then, after establishing it as fiction, Welles stepped aside and let the players begin the production.

Or maybe if listeners had read the newspaper listing of the program—"Today, 8:00–9:00 P.M. Play: H. G. Wells, War of the Worlds–WABC"—they would have known it was fiction.

Or maybe if they had listened carefully to the three announcements during the broadcast that emphasized the program's fictional nature, they would have known it was just a work of drama.

But they didn't. Instead they panicked—and in a massive way.

Once the initial announcement was made, the rest of the broadcast was written in such a way as to simulate a regular radio show, a format that would make listeners believe it was true, or at least not question it. Welles thought it would add more drama that way, but, quite frankly, the cast thought the whole production was boring and dull. The dramatization started with a fictional government weather report that began, "For the next twenty-four hours not much change in temperature from a slight atmospheric disturbance of undetermined origin is reported . . ." and then supposedly the broadcast shifted to the Meridian Room of the Park Plaza Hotel in New York City. Listeners thought they were hearing a real band, the Ramon

Raquello Orchestra, playing. After twenty or thirty seconds of music, the program was interrupted by an announcer from the fictional Intercontinental Radio News. The announcer began, "Ladies and gentlemen, we interrupt this program of dance music to bring you a special bulletin. . . . Twenty minutes before eight, central time, Professor Farrell of the Mt. Jennings Observatory, Chicago, Illinois, reports observing several explosions of incandescent gas occurring at regular intervals on the planet Mars. The spectroscope indicates the gas to be hydrogen and moving towards the earth with enormous velocity."

The program then switched back to the music in progress in the Meridian Room. An announcement was made saying that the orchestra was getting ready to play "a tune that never loses its flavor . . . 'Little White Lies'"—a convenient little joke thrown in by Orson Welles.

After a few seconds of "Little White Lies," the music was interrupted again by a slightly more frantic news bulletin and an interview with a Professor Pierson by news reporter Carl Phillips. Phillips had the professor reassure the public that there was nothing to worry about in regard to the gases that had been reported as escaping earlier in the broadcast, that Mars was over 40 million miles away. The professor then gave his opinion with a chuckle, "I assure you there is no life on Mars." As he concluded his statement, the professor was handed an urgent message that the reporter read to the listening public. The message told of a large shock that had been felt at the Wilmuth farm in Grovers Mill, New Jersey. Both the professor and the reporter said they were headed over there and would report to the public once at the site. In the meantime, back to the music.

This was the pattern for the first seven minutes of the broadcast, appearing to happen in real time. The Meridian Room was then finally ditched, and the entire broadcast moved to the scene of the invasion. Carl Phillips was "on the scene" giving an eyewitness account, conducting interviews with "townspeople" who had witnessed the landing, "scientists" who were giving their opinions on what this object was, and "military men" who were talking about defensive strategies in the event they were necessary. All the while sirens and crowd noises could be heard in the background.

It seemed so real and was easily believable back then because listeners were used to getting their news in that format: programming, interruption, back to programming. Only the observant would have noticed that the Columbia Broadcasting censors had made sure the names of certain institutions, such as the Signal Corps of the New Jersey State Militia, were fictional so they wouldn't be confused with actual government or scientific organizations. But those small details were forgotten as a sense of panic started to grow.

The program really began to cause hysteria when Phillips began to describe the silver object that had landed as 30 yards wide but then suddenly stopped midsentence. As the object began to open, he yelled, "Wait—this is the most terrifying thing I have ever witnessed! Someone or something is crawling out of the metal cylinder . . . it looks like . . . a gray snake and another and another . . . the face is indescribable . . . the eyes are black . . . a tentacled creature with saliva dripping from rimless lips. The police are waving a flag of truce . . . giant flames . . . Good Lord . . ."—then sounds of lasers and bombs were heard—"It's coming this way . . . only 20 yards . . ."

Then the broadcast line went dead. An announcer told people to stay calm as they looked into the technical difficulties. A few minutes later a bulletin came in saying the charred body of Carl Phillips had been found and that forty people were dead.

By this time New Jersey listeners believed they were being attacked in their own backyard and were desperately trying to figure out how to escape. And since this was a national broadcast, those in the surrounding areas of New York, Philadelphia, and Boston began to panic as well.

People tied up the phone lines, calling friends, family, and neighbors to warn them that Earth was being invaded. Parents with students in Princeton called and ordered them to come home. It was like Chicken Little yelling the sky was falling—news spread quickly. The American Telephone Company said volume went up 39 percent during the broadcast and continued for an hour after that.

The police stations were flooded with panicked calls. People's imaginations ran wild—some claimed they'd actually seen the "little green men from Mars." Some described the invasion to police in detail. One woman called and exclaimed, "You can't imagine the horror of it! It's hell!" A man told a policeman, "I went to the roof, and I could see the smoke from the bombs drifting over toward New York. What shall I do?" Police tried to calm each frantic caller. But there were thousands.

The only citizen who seemed undaunted by this all was a Mr. Anderson, one of the actual tenants of the Wilson farm (called the Wilmuth farm in the broadcast). Mrs. Anderson ran to wake up her husband to tell him about the invasion. Farmer Anderson got up, went outside to the front porch, heard croaking toads and chirping crickets, and said, "Darn fools," and went back to sleep.

But he was only one of the few who remained calm during this prank. The other calm souls were the Mercury Theatre Players themselves, totally unaware of the hysteria they were causing. They just kept on acting out bulletin after bulletin.

Upping the intensity, the radio station proceeded to claim that the airwaves were being taken over by state militia in Trenton to describe the scene further. A Patton-like military man got on and said, "There are 7,000 armed men closing in on an old metal tube." He exuded confidence that his men would destroy the invaders. But then something went wrong. The old metal tube fired, destroying all but 120 men. A report came in stating that they had just witnessed the most startling defeat ever suffered by an army in modern times.

Meanwhile, off the air, people were emptying apartment buildings, dragging belongings into their cars, and bottle-necking main arteries like the Penn's Neck and Brunswick Turnpike (Route 1). Some people in Dutch Neck were literally on their hands and knees in the streets, praying for salvation. Others ran into churches screaming, "The world is coming to an end!" One man was rushed to the hospital because he had a heart attack from the stress.

The broadcast continued: "Poisonous black smoke from the Jersey marshes . . . gas masks useless . . . urge population to move into the open spaces." People dutifully ran through the streets with towels covering their faces or called the police department to ask how to avoid the poison.

Fictitious news flashes poured in fast and furious: France and England were offering their support; the air force and army had tried again to destroy the invaders but were wiped out; people were dropping like flies.

There seemed to be no hope. Then, just as the continent was toppling into oblivion, the real announcer cut in to once again remind listeners that this was a dramatization—but to deaf ears. Millions were already out on the streets, trying to save themselves and loved ones.

The hysteria, most intense in New Jersey, created by this Halloween broadcast was not known in the United States since the news of the Great War.

Not everyone was a doomsayer though. One Princeton student tried to use the destruction of Earth to his gambling advantage. He actually called the police to ask if they knew if "Coach Ted Wieman's players had been stricken by the poison gas." He wanted to know before placing a bet on Saturday's upcoming game.

At the conclusion of the hour, the broadcast ended with Orson Welles saying, "We couldn't soap your windows or steal your garden gates so we annihilated the world before your very ears. . . . This is our version of dressing up in a sheet and jumping out of the bushes and saying 'Boo' . . . and if your doorbell rings and nobody's there, that was no Martian, it's Halloween." The players then headed home, only to find out about the pandemonium they'd caused.

Immediately the radio station ran several announcements assuring people that what they'd heard was not real. So much for a dull presentation.

The next day the *New York Times* headline read "Radio Listeners in Panic, Taking War Drama as Fact." The *Trenton Evening Times* stated "Hoax Spreads Terror Here, Some Pack Up." The Trenton paper further stated "U.S. Board Starts Probe as Protests Mark Panic Spread by Radio Drama."

And probe they did. A new ruling stated that radio announcements of special bulletins must be broadcast in such a manner that people know they're true.

Some papers criticized Welles for performing such a hoax, saying it was irresponsible; others said he was a genius, pointing out how the power of the media had gotten out of hand.

Today a plaque stands in Grovers Mill marking the spot of the "Martian invasion" and states, "For a brief time as many as one million people throughout the country believed that Martians had invaded the earth, beginning with Grovers Mill, New Jersey." The plaque commemorates the most terrifying and greatest Halloween trick to ever scare a nation.

The Accidental Invention

· 1938 ·

They say sometimes accidents happen for a reason, and in this case an accident that occurred in a lab changed the lives of culinary chefs worldwide and astronauts in outer space. What was that accident? The invention of Teflon.

Roy J. Plunkett was born in New Carlisle, Ohio, in 1910. After graduating with a B.A. from Manchester College, he quickly moved up the educational ladder and gained a Ph.D. from Ohio State University; his specialty was chemistry. His first postdoctoral position was with the famous DuPont Company—not a bad start for a recent graduate.

Plunkett's first assignment for the company was as a research chemist at its Jackson Laboratory in Deepwater. He was asked to work on synthesizing new forms of the DuPont refrigerant Freon. He was thrilled to be working for such a prestigious company, and he took great pride in his work.

Plunkett moved along methodically until that fateful and lucky day of April 6, 1938. On this day the twenty-seven-year-old chemist and his technician assistant, Jack Relak, were just two of a large group of scientists who were studying and testing the chemical reactions of the refrigerant gas known as tetrafluroethylene, or TFE for short. It was work as usual.

As they had done many times before, they were testing and documenting the results of their experiment. Just as things were running smoothly, they noticed that one pressurized cylinder of gas, which they had filled themselves, had failed to discharge when its valve was opened. They set aside what they thought was an empty chamber and continued with their scheduled experiments.

At the end of the day, as they were about to get rid of the faulty cylinder, Relak noticed it was too heavy to be empty. He suggested they cut it open to see what had gone wrong. Plunkett agreed, even though they both knew there was a great chance of explosion due to the nature of the gas. As they cautiously opened the faulty chamber, they discovered that for some reason the gas inside the chamber had mysteriously solidified into a waxy white powder. As Plunkett wrote in his laboratory notebook, "a white, solid material which was supposed to be a polymerized product of the Freon compound" was inside. They were perplexed. What the heck was this thing? Because its chemical composition was unknown, this new product was issued a laboratory code number: K416.

Being a true scientist, Plunkett was extremely curious. He put aside his scheduled work and decided to test this mysterious K416. His mind wouldn't rest until he could figure out exactly what it was.

Plunkett worked late into the night, and after a series of tests, he could see that it was much more lubricant than other slippery solids, like graphite for instance. (It was so slippery that it couldn't even stick to itself and had to be applied as a coating mixed with other chemicals.) This substance, which had formed into what is known as a polytetrafluoroethylene (PTFE), was inert, which basically means it showed a complete indifference to attack by any and all chemicals—it was like the superman of chemicals. Plus it could withstand temperatures from 450 to 725 degrees Fahrenheit. Heat could pass through it at those temperatures without melting it. Plunkett was fascinated. His mind raced with the potential of this substance. Here he had the world's most slippery solid, which could hold together in a vacuum, something that would be priceless in outer space. Plunkett wanted to see just how far he could push this newfound substance.

For the next few days, he was in overdrive. Putting his scheduled work aside, he kept testing the limits of the substance. Plunkett found that the molecules in the gas had bonded and made a resin. This unique resin acted like an impenetrable shield, which protected its own atoms. Immediately seeing the potential for this, Plunkett started to work on ways to reproduce it in the lab. He did, and since he was working for DuPont, it became the company's property.

The polymer substance became known and trademarked as Teflon, and Dr. Roy Plunkett and his accidental invention became known the world over. Plunkett was inducted into the Plastics Hall of Fame, next to such inventors as Thomas Edison, Louis Pasteur, and the Wright Brothers.

In 1946 the first Teflon products went on the market as machine parts for military and industrial applications. Today Teflon is used in over forty countries around the world for various things. Its number of applications is remarkable. The very same cookware coater that Emeril Lagasse and Julia Child whip up their culinary delights in was also used on the space suits that allowed men to walk on the Moon. Teflon coated the outer layer of their suits and also lined the systems used to carry liquid oxygen during the Apollo flights in the late 1960s and 1970s. It was additionally used in heat shields for rocket reentry and wire insulation.

Others soon saw the amazing aspects of Teflon and found that it was very stretchable and had tiny holes, therefore allowing water droplets in. Breathable, waterproof cloth like Gore-Tex, which is stretched Teflon applied over a fabric, was invented. Teflon also coats lightbulbs, electrical wires and chemical tanks and is even used on Lady Liberty, acting as a corrosion-prevention insulator applied between her copper skin and the inner stainless steel framework. It's even used in sports, in the fiberglass roof of the Silverdome in Michigan. Today it's a household word and is sometimes used to describe someone who seems to be able to avoid blame or evade the law, such as the deceased New York Mob boss John Gotti, who was known as the "Teflon Don" before he was finally convicted.

Scientists have been quoted as saying that the invention of Teflon is "an example of serendipity, a flash of genius, a lucky accident . . . even a mixture of all three." Plunkett knew its value on that 1938 day in the lab in New Jersey, and he was smart enough to realize that Teflon could be used in ways that are "only limited by the imagination." One thing is for sure—it's no imagination that the small accident in the Jersey lab revolutionized the plastics industry and provided limitless benefits to mankind. Omelette anyone?

A Humdinger of an Explosion
·1965·

U ntil the early twentieth century, astronomers believed that there were three possible explanations for the creation of the universe. The first theory said that the universe was static, meaning that the mutual gravitational pull of stars and planets kept everything together in one uniform space. In other words, the universe never started and is never going to end. Einstein supported this static theory with his theory of relativity.

The second theory said that the universe oscillated, meaning it was like one giant cosmic balloon forever contracting and expanding. For a few billion years it would inflate, and then, when it was about to burst and expand into nothingness, the gravitational pull of the planets would pull everything back in reverse and the universe would crash onto itself, creating heat and light. The heat and light would cause it to expand outward again, and it would continue in this yo-yo fashion indefinitely. The oscillating model said the universe had exploded many times. Einstein commented, "This circumstance [of an expanding universe] irritates me."

The third theory said that the universe could be open. This theory was a bit more complicated and paradoxical and therefore the hardest for scientists to believe. It stated that all the universe's matter and energy at one time was contained in a single tiny stable glowing fiery dot that sat in space for eternity until it reached ten billion degrees Fahrenheit and exploded. But this theory didn't make sense, for if only a single object was there, it was at rest and not constantly building. If nothing else existed, what outside force could cause it to explode? Unless, of course, something like a supernatural creator kicked the universe into being with *one* gigantic bang, a bang that occurred in a matter of minutes and would reverberate for sixteen billion years with a low hum.

Scientists did not want to believe this third theory—it seemed to go against all scientific logic and would confirm that the universe was "created" all at once by someone or something. Most chose to ignore the theory. But in 1965, when two New Jersey Bell Labs scientists proved to the world that the third theory was probably correct, scientists could no longer ignore it. Their discovery changed the way modern science viewed the cosmic world.

In 1960 Bell Labs built a giant antenna on Crawford Hill in Holmdel. This 20-foot-tall horn reflector was part of a transmission system called Echo, which would amplify weak radio signals, bounce them off large metallic balloons, and send them long distances. The Echo system was booked commercially for a long time. When the more advanced Telstar satellite system came in, the Echo system went out.

Two Bell Labs radio astronomers had their eye on the Holmdel horn antenna, and they each had similar reasons for wanting to use it. In 1965, when Echo was no longer the transmission system du jour, they both jumped on the opportunity.

Arno Penzias was a German radio astronomer born in 1933. He had done his Ph.D. dissertation on MASERS (microwave amplification by stimulated emission of radiation). Basically, he was looking for a way to amplify and measure radio signals from the spaces between galaxies, and he knew the horn antenna would make a great radio telescope and would be just the instrument he needed to continue his observations. Robert Wilson also had used MASERS to amplify and map weak radio signals from the Milky Way. The two men saw they had similar interests and began to use the antenna as a telescope.

Unfortunately, there was a very annoying background "noise"—an irritating three degree Kelvin (3K) hum that sounded like static on the radio—picked up by the antenna. No one was really shocked at the noise since everyone assumed it came from the telescope itself, which was not unusual. Since it hadn't interfered with the Echo system's operation, no one had ever bothered to "fix" the noise. But Penzias and Wilson needed to get rid of the noise in order to make the observations they'd planned.

They first wanted to measure the characteristics of the hum. Like a doctor examining a patient, they took notes on all its symptoms. They noticed the hum was a uniform signal. It was in the microwave range length of 7 centimeters, which normally would have a low intensity, but this hum was a hundred times more intense than expected for that wavelength. And the noise seemed to be coming from all over the sky, night and day, during all four seasons. It was like an annoying fly on a hot summer night that lands on your ear every time you try to go to sleep.

The two astronomers began to try to swat out the noise. They wanted to rule out every possible source of the radiation. They pointed the antenna at New York City, but it wasn't urban interference causing the problem. They tested to see if the sound was radiation from our galaxy or extraterrestrial radio sources, but it wasn't. They even thought it might be the pigeons using the antenna as a penthouse. They chased them out and cleaned up their droppings only to find it wasn't for the birds. Since the sound was there during all four seasons, they realized it couldn't be coming from the solar system. They even debated whether it was fallout from a 1962 above-ground nuclear test, but realized that the fallout would have caused a decrease, not an increase, in the noise.

With every option exhausted, they concluded that it wasn't

the machine and it wasn't some random noise, but that it was coming from outside the galaxy. Unfortunately, they knew of no radio source that would account for it. They were determined to find the answer so they could get on with their long-awaited observations. So they turned to theoretical explanations.

At the same time 40 miles away, three Princeton University astrophysicists by the names of Robert Dicke, Jim Peebles, and David Wilkenson were elaborating on the theory of the big bang. Dicke suggested that if there was indeed a big bang, the explosion would cause a residue that would last for billions of years in the form of a low-level background noise at a volume of 5K. They say timing is everything. Dicke and gang were just about to publish a paper about the possibility of finding this radiation sound. Since word travels fast in the scientific community, Wilson and Penzias found out about the unpublished paper. They telephoned Dicke's group and invited them to listen to their 3K humming noise. They had found a match. Dicke commented to his fellow researchers, "We've been scooped."

The two groups decided to publish their results at the same time. Both rushed off letters to the *Astrophysical Journal Letters*. Dicke and associates outlined the importance of cosmic background noise to support the big bang theory. Wilson, who had been weaned on the static universe theory, felt uncomfortable with these findings, so he and Penzias stuck to "just the facts" in their letter, titled "A Measurement of Excess Temperature at 4,080 Megacycles per Second." They put an extra note in saying that the possible explanation of the noise they found might be given in Dicke's companion letter. A Harvard physicist named Edward Purcell read the letter and commented, "This just may be the most important thing that anybody has ever seen."

The ironic thing was that these two groups weren't the first to hear this static noise, they were just the first to investigate it and piece it all together. It was heard in the 1950s when "the study of the universe was not the sort of thing to which a respectable scientist would devote his time to." Good thing these two groups didn't follow the norm.

Like it or not, as much as scientists tried to deny the big bang theory, the phenomenon that Penzias and Wilson had stumbled on, the measurement of "cosmic background radiation (CBR)," combined with results from Edwin Hubble's telescope, which showed that the galaxies are rushing away, made a very strong case for the theory. This sent the scientific community into a panic. Their static model was dead. Mathematicians, physicists, and astronomers joined forces to try to prove that theory number two, the oscillating model, was the right one. They wanted evidence of the eternity of the universe.

Dr. Robert Jastrow, the greatest astrophysicist of the time, headed the project. For thirteen years Jastrow and his team tried to find proof to back the second theory. They couldn't. In 1978 Jastrow released a NASA definitive report that shocked the public with his announcement that the open model, the big bang theory, was correct. He wrote in the *New York Times,* "This is an exceedingly strange development, unexpected by all but the theologians. They have always accepted the word of the Bible: 'In the beginning God created heaven and earth . . .' (But) for the scientist, who has lived by his faith in the power of reason, the story ends like a bad dream. He has scaled the mountains of ignorance; he is about to conquer the highest peak; (and) as he pulls himself over the final rock, he is greeted by a band of theologians who have been sitting there for centuries."

That same year, 1978, Arno Penzias and Robert Wilson's findings earned them the Nobel Prize in Physics for changing an "unlimited theoretical speculation into one disciplined by direct observation."

They provided the evidence that confirmed George Gamow and Abbe Georges Lamaitre's "Big Bang Theory" by presenting "the most dramatic support ever" for the open universe. Of course there are always the die-hard scientists who believe that new evidence will appear and overturn this "created universe" theory.

As Wilson later said about his findings at the New Jersey lab, "At that time, it certainly wasn't clear that the reflector was going to lead to something as important as information on the origin of the universe." But indeed it did. The faint whispers the antenna picked up were the leftovers from an explosion sixteen billion years ago that created the universe.

Today the proof of the Big Bang theory discovered by two New Jersey scientists is the "standard model" for how the universe was formed. The site of the horn antenna was designated as a National Historic Landmark in 1990. And, indeed, it should be since that discovery is considered the most important discovery in 500 years of modern astronomy. Such a big theory from such a small town . . .

Nice going, New Jersey.

Lucy's New Home
· 1970 ·

She'd been standing in the same spot for eighty-nine years—but Lucy the Elephant was about to get a new home.

Lucy was born in 1881 when a twenty-five-year-old real estate developer, James V. Lafferty, who was also an engineer and inventor, came into possession of a few sandy lots in the South Atlantic City/Margate area. At that time the area was filled with scrub pine, dune grass, bayberry bushes, and a few fishing shacks. Lafferty couldn't get to the property during high tide because of a deep tidal creek nearby. His land was far from the beaten path of horse-drawn streetcars and the houses in the area. What was he to do with a bunch of remote sandy lots? How could he get people to come to the area and purchase the land?

Lafferty knew he needed something that would gather press and attention. Something so big that people would come just to gawk. So he decided to build an elephant! When people came to view the creature, he'd hit them with his real estate sales pitch, suggesting that the area was perfect for a summer cottage.

To set his plan in motion, Lafferty hired a Philadelphia architect by the name of William Free. Lafferty then applied for a patent on his elephant design. His application stated, "My invention consists of a building in the form of an animal, the body of which is floored and divided into rooms. . . . The legs contain the stairs that lead to the body. . . . and it may be in the form of any other animal than an elephant, as that of a fish, fowl, etc." The last part protected him in case anyone tried to steal his idea. If someone wanted to build a giant otter using Lafferty's method, that person would have to pay him royalties. The government granted the patent on December 5, 1882; it was good for seventeen years.

Lafferty stuck with his original plan—an elephant. The elephant was designed after a picture he had seen in an adventure magazine of P. T. Barnum's Jumbo the Elephant from the exotic land of British Raj. Upon completion, Lucy stood facing the ocean. There are stories of many a sailor who spotted her while making their way up the coast, doing a double take through their telescopes only to realize that it really was a giant elephant!

And what a giant she was. Lucy stood in a feeding position, upright on all fours with her trunk down. She was six stories tall and weighed ninety tons, making her the world's largest elephant. (Good thing no one had to feed her!) She was 38 feet long and 80 feet in circumference. Her head was 16 feet long, her neck 6 feet, her legs and tusks 22 feet, and her tail 26 feet, and her glass eyes (which also serve as windows) were 18 inches in diameter. Her ears alone weighed 2,000 pounds—not even Dumbo's ears were that big! It took more than a million pieces of wood and 200 kegs of nails to create all her curves. Four tons of bolts and bars were used to keep her firmly in place. Twelve thousand square feet of tin fashioned her "skin." Some say Lucy could be seen from 8 miles away, without binoculars.

Lafferty claimed that Lucy cost $38,000 to build once all was said and done—a huge chunk of money at the time.

Lucy was accessible via two doors in her hind legs: one an entrance, the other an exit. Once inside, visitors climbed a spiral staircase to a large reception room. From there they could access other rooms on that floor. From the belly of the beast, guests could look out one of the twenty-two windows for their viewing pleasure. For the grand finale, a visitor could climb onto Lucy's back and into her howdah (the canopied seat used to ride the back of an elephant) and view the entire Atlantic City/Margate area.

Once the pachyderm was built, Lafferty started a publicity campaign by placing ads in New Jersey and Philadelphia newspapers: "ELEPHANT BAZAAR, South Atlantic City—this remarkable structure is the only one in the world built in this novel form." Then he snuck in his sales pitch: "Lots for sale on installments . . . in this fast booming South Atlantic City."

Word spread, and Lucy eventually became internationally known. There was no official opening ceremony, and no admission fee was charged. She was simply used as a ploy to get people to come to the area. Lafferty was thrilled with the response. Lucy made loads of money for her owner, and he went on to build two other, even larger, elephants: "The Light of Asia" in South Cape May (that elephant was eventually torn down) and "The Elephantine Colossus" at Coney Island (this elephant later burned down). Unfortunately, while all three were standing, Lafferty overextended himself financially and had to sell Lucy. He found a willing buyer in John Gertzen of Philadelphia.

Behind Lucy, Gertzen built a Turkish pavilion with slot machines and horse-racing grounds. According to legend, it was his wife, Sophia Gertzen, who named the elephant "Lucy." The Gertzen family took care of Lucy through a series of changes.

For a while Lucy was a tourist attraction, then a private summer home. Some incorrect accounts say she was a hotel. She was heavily damaged in a storm in 1903 and had to be dug out of sand up to her knees. That must have upset her, because she turned to drinking. Lucy became a tavern. She was almost turned to ashes by the flick of an ill-tossed cigarette. Finally, Sophia turned Lucy into the main attraction of a tourist camp. People could tent at her feet and get a visit inside Lucy for a small admission fee. Several famous people came to visit Lucy's innards, including President and Mrs. Woodrow Wilson, the Duponts, and Henry Ford. When the tent city became too large, Sophia was forced to close it down.

Eventually the booze and the weather did Lucy in. By the late 1970s she was a wreck. Her creator, Lafferty, and caretakers, the Gertzens, were dead. The Gertzens' descendants donated Lucy to the city of Margate, sold the land on which she stood, and retired to Florida. Lucy was all alone, staring out to sea, just wilting.

The citizens of Margate took pity on Lucy and put her back on the right track. The Margate Civic Association restored her to her original beauty with a complete facial and makeover. They decided she needed a change of scenery, and in a heavily publicized, carefully planned event on July 20, 1970, they moved the six-story behemoth 2 blocks to her new home.

Onlookers and movers assembled at the site at seven o'clock in the morning. An architect examined Lucy and pronounced her in good health, saying she could be moved without damage. But then a heavy fog rolled in. This put a dent in their plans, and everyone stood around drinking coffee, anxiously waiting.

At nine o'clock the fog started to clear, and the foreman shouted, "Let 'er roll!" A whistle blew, and a small yellow pickup pulled Lucy down the street. The crowd speculated on whether the small truck was up to the job of pulling the ninety-ton elephant. Since all this took place near Atlantic City, perhaps at least some gamblers placed side bets.

Cameras clicked, reporters filmed, and children watched in awe. At one point the tiny truck had to go over a curb on Cedar Grove Avenue. Lucy creaked and groaned (give her a break—after all, she hadn't moved in over eighty-nine years). The crowd was silent, praying that their elephant—a large part of the area's history—wouldn't tip over. Police cars flashing their lights led the way, and the telephone company dropped wires to allow Lucy to pass without harm. Spectators cheered and applauded as Lucy passed by. It was a very proud moment for her.

Albert Ranalli, the head honcho in charge of the moving project, commented, "The only thing that could equal this [move] would be to move the Sphinx from the Valley to the Nile."

Seven hours after beginning her trip, Lucy was safely planted in her new home. A year later she became the only elephant in America designated as a National Historic Landmark.

Restoration has made Lucy a beautiful sight to behold. Her restorers brought her back to her original self as closely as possible. When they analyzed her innards, they found some peculiar stuff. Margaret Westfield, Lucy's restoration architect, said, "One of the most interesting things when matching the original plaster composition was that it had rice holes and loose cotton in it [apparently in an effort to make it lighter] and was tinted gastric pink all the way through."

Today tourists can visit Lucy at 9200 Atlantic Avenue in Margate. For a small fee, they can go inside and buy postcards, view artifacts, or climb onto her back for a view of the Atlantic Ocean and the old site where she used to stand. And if you pay close attention, you might notice a little secret: Lucy is actually a boy! Either way, one thing's for certain, Lucy makes for one heck of a good snapshot.

A Roll of the Dice
· 1978 ·

Atlantic City had made a name for itself by building the world's first boardwalk in 1879, so businessmen wouldn't have to deal with all that pesky sand, and then by having a bathing beauty "mermaid" contest in 1921, now known as the first Miss America Pageant. As the city grew, it became a hotspot for entertainers, and people from all over the world came to visit the "Queen of the Coast." But after World War II the Queen lost her crown, and the love affair with Atlantic City ended. The city lost its shine and people lost interest—and there went the tourists and their revenue.

The townspeople were anxious to try something, anything, to revive the city. That something became another New Jersey first and made history. On May 26, 1978, the Resorts Casino opened its doors and became the first casino and gaming mecca in the United States outside of Nevada. The gamble they took in opening such an establishment took Atlantic City's estimated $316 million in real estate and turned it into multi-billion-dollar property. This truly was a unique tool of urban development.

But how did it all begin? Bringing in a casino was discussed in 1966, but the idea was rejected. Then, in November of 1976, New Jersey voters (convinced by a well-financed promotional campaign) overwhelmingly endorsed gambling in New Jersey as an experiment to try to revive Atlantic City. The Casino Control Act was signed. Resorts International stepped up to the plate and renovated the fifty-year-old Chalfonte Haddon Hotel into a fifty-million-dollar casino. The president of the company, Jack Davis, gave this promise to New Jersey: "This first casino east of Las Vegas will bring credit to Atlantic City and the state, and we will have the highest integrity of any jurisdiction in the world since we know the entire world will be watching to see if [casino gambling] will reach its goals."

To make all this a reality, the State Casino Control Commission had several obstacles to overcome. Resorts International had to convince the commission that it and its operators were not involved in organized crime. An eighteen-month-long investigation was conducted. Everyone from the hotel-casino executives and employees on down to any person who worked with one of the company's 338 affiliates was suspect. In one case, someone even allowed his home to be searched without a warrant just so he could get a dealer's license. The state wanted to make sure the money was going in its pockets, not the mob's. The casino was granted a temporary license to operate, even though the investigations were still going on when the doors officially opened.

The commission worked up until fifteen hours and fifteen minutes prior to the opening ceremonies. They passed through liquor licenses, several hundred service-industry submissions, bar passes, and even requirements on the slot machines, such as whether all of the machines needed to have a least five separate dials and blinking lights. They had to decide on minimum bets at the craps and blackjack tables and at the roulette wheels—which caused a big commotion since they approved regulations that discouraged the small bettor, with a minimum at the baccarat table, for example, being $20 at all times.

Everything was decided in favor of the casino, giving it the "go" plus a one-year monopoly on gambling in Atlantic City. They had everything they needed to legally open the doors on May 26 at ten o'clock, exactly two years to the day after Resorts had proposed the deal, marking the beginning of gambling history.

The final fifteen hours before the opening found the casino in a whirlwind. All 1,016 employees (40 percent women and 43 percent minorities) were on hand attending to every detail. And there were many last-minute details to take care of for this historic event. Carpenters and electricians hammered and wired, painters put finishing touches on the rooms with 1930s decor, and hotel employees were drilled on the behavior codes: "Don't say 'You look tired.'" "Don't say 'Yeah' or 'O.K.' or 'All right.' "Don't use vulgar language." And "Don't stare!"

There was also the major matter of security and safety. Atlantic City is located on Absecon Island in Atlantic County, a community only 48 blocks long and 10 blocks wide. It's 60 miles southeast of Philadelphia, and 100 miles from New York City. It was estimated that 400,000 cars from all over would try to cram themselves on that little island, and since there were only 50,000 parking spots, that could be a problem.

The night before the official opening there was a "special Thursday night show" for 1,100 invited VIP guests consisting of state officials and resort personalities, featuring sexy showgirls and Ms. Singleton, the star of the popular movie *Blondie*. Up until show time some cast members picketed outside the hotel, protesting their low wages. Some were making only $117 per week, which wasn't enough to live on, as opposed to the union requirement of $350 per week. The union and the hotel were trying to work it out. None of the VIPs inside knew about the picketing, but the police were on hand to make sure it didn't turn nasty. The hotel's entertainment producer, Tibor Rudas, was not upset though. He said that in a worse case scenario, Steve Lawrence and Eydie Gorme, a famous Vegas singing couple who had opened many hotels around the country, would go on and perform if the cast didn't. But true to the heart of every entertainer, the cast knew the show must go on. They came in at nine o'clock, the show went on without a hitch, and 1,100 VIPs left very happy.

The next morning was a dreary and rainy day—but spirits could not be dampened. At exactly ten o'clock, with celebrities, politicians, invited guests, and about 20,000 people (much lower than estimated) on hand ready to place their bets, a ribbon-cutting ceremony was underway.

Governor Byrne, a big supporter of legalized gambling, cut the pumpkin-colored ribbon on the gaming room floor, saying, "My father always told me never to bet on anything but Notre Dame and the Yankees, but for anyone not willing to take my father's advice, I now declare this casino open." With that, the crowds rushed in. They were greeted with flashy colored walls, a Victorian flair, and green-felted card and dice tables. The casino was humming with the sound of shiny new slot machines. Dealers barked out, "Come on, folks, place your bets!" Cigar and cigarette smoke and the scent of money filled the air.

Security guards were ready to limit access to the casino area if it became dangerously overcrowded. There were close to a hundred hidden ceiling cameras encased in silver bubbles that fed to a video room where the gamblers' every move could be captured.

The "honor" of the first $10 lost went to Steve Lawrence, half of the famed singing duo. The loss came at the craps table when Lawrence rolled a five but then rolled a seven before he could get another five, making him probably one of the most famous $10 losers in history.

The first major winners were Max and Hilda Kleiman of Baltimore, who didn't even come to Atlantic City to gamble. They had come for the national convention of the Association of Parents of American-Israelis. They stopped by the casino just to kill time and stuck five quarters into a machine, and two winning rows of black bars showed through the window. They won a jackpot of $125 but had to work a little for their prize money since the machine only paid out $50. Mr. Kleiman had to track down a house attendant to pay him off while his wife guarded the machine. She promptly led her husband out of the casino with the money in her purse. No one's sure if they ever wound up going to their meeting.

While the Kleimans walked out, others patiently waited on the boardwalk to get in. One man stated, "I wouldn't have missed this. This is something to tell your grandchildren."

The optimistic crowds weren't the only eager ones. Some of the dealers who had just graduated dealer school the previous Monday were standing ready for the onslaught of people. One dealer, a Mr. Borino, wearing an ill-fitting tuxedo and standing behind a blackjack table, said, "We're excited. A lot of us here were out of work." Then his well-manicured hands dealt out the first round to two guys named Tom and Fred Maul, both wearing aviator-style glasses. Joining them at the table were a female producer of the *Today* television show and a man wearing Lions Club insignia clothes. In the first round played, Tom lost, Fred won, and the television producer had blackjack.

After the first hour, smoke lay over the room like a cheap toupee, and the casino was well broken in.

Today Atlantic City has become known the world over as a first-rate casino/gaming mecca. It has thirteen casinos that collectively pay out an average of $97 million to visitors every day. Each and every visitor goes there wishing for the triumph of hope over reason that goes hand-in-hand with fighting the odds and quick returns. Some go home happy, some go home sad, but usually everyone comes back.

But Atlantic City is the real winner in all of this, having taken a big gamble that turned the city into one of "America's Favorite Playgrounds." The experiment was a big success, and to this day Lady Luck seems to be on the city's side.

New Jersey's Guinness Record
· 1992 ·

The Museum of American Glass, located in Millville, is the largest museum in the country dedicated to preserving the history of glass made in the United States. It houses over 6,500 pieces in its collection. With all that glass, how could any piece stand out above the others? Well, there is one way. One glass stands 7 feet, 8 inches tall—taller than any National Basketball Association player. It's the *Guinness Book of World Records'* largest bottle and has the capacity to hold 188 gallons of liquid. Talk about a big drink of water!

Now this bottle isn't like any of the other finds at the museum. This record-setting bottle was created on September 26, 1992, during a weekend celebration event called Glass Blast. It was the grand finale of all the events and demonstrations and was created by the internationally renowned glass artist Steven Tobin and his team in the museum's own glass-making studio.

Glassmaking, tomatoes, the Jersey Shore, the Jersey Turnpike, and the Pinelands are all a big part of the state, and New Jerseyans like to celebrate their heritage. During the Glass Blast weekend, they wanted to celebrate the tradition of South Jersey glassmaking, a tradition that goes back to the days when the colonists were forbidden to manufacture glass products so they would be forced to buy them from England. But the colonists were resourceful. One man, Caspar Wistar, found that the silica sand in southern New Jersey was an excellent sand for making glass, and the remoteness of the area made it easy to hide the operation of glassmaking from the Mother Country.

So the secret production of functional glass such as window panes, bottles, jars, sugar bowls, and cream jugs continued on the sly for forty years. Many German immigrants came to work for Wistar in Alloway in 1739. When the secret glass factory closed in 1777, many of the employees started their own factories and laid the foundation for the glass industry that flourished. With the help of skilled immigrants from England, Ireland, France, Belgium, and Italy in the nineteenth and twentieth centuries, more than 200 glass factories were established in New Jersey. To celebrate this heritage, Glass Blast organizers wanted something memorable, something that would stand out, something that would make the event spectacular. What better way than to set a world record?

The museum sent out brochures inviting everyone to celebrate glass heritage: "Not only will you be able to see a team of glassblowers attempt to blow the world's largest glass bottle, but you will be able to hear some of the finest musicians performing regional and ethnic music and dance. You can browse in the all glass flea market, watch craft demonstrations, see videos . . . see neon sign making . . . and sample some food from other countries." Everyone was excited. Not only were they attempting to set a world record, but they were also attempting to beat a previous record that had been set in 1904—a bottle able to hold 108 gallons that was made at the Whitall Tatum Glass Factory and displayed at the St. Louis World's Fair. Unfortunately, the bottle had broken in transit, and only a picture of the team of men who created it with the bottle towering over them still exists.

Glassmaking takes skill. If things are not done at just the right time the glass sculpture can be ruined. To get ready for this world record, Steven Tobin and his team consisting of Dale

Leader, Daisuke Shintani, Don Friel, David Lewin, and Chuck Smart practiced for months. They had to utilize every glass-blowing technique developed and create a few of their own to be able to pull it off. As Tobin said, "It has been an education for all of us."

With the big day upon them, they were ready. At the T. C. Wheaton Glass Factory in Wheaton Village in Millville, the team worked with precision as curious onlookers watched from behind a partition. Each team member had a specific job.

The first step in blowing glass is to place a stainless-steel $4^1/_2$-foot-long blowpipe onto the ledge of a furnace that is filled with red-hot molten glass. The glassblower has to be extremely careful while near the furnace since it is a scorching 2,200 degrees Fahrenheit—or, to put it in perspective, ten times hotter than boiling water. The pipe is tilted at a forty-five-degree angle, dipped into the liquid, and then rotated to get a gather of glass, which looks like a blob of honey. The gather has to be continuously rotated to keep the shape consistent. Then the gather is pulled out of the furnace at that same forty-five-degree angle. The pipe is then leveled with this "gather" of glass on it.

Once the first gather was on, one of the glassblowers blew down the hollow blowpipe to create a small bubble of air inside the glass. They let it cool for a few seconds. Timing was critical—each second the glass becomes cooler and harder to manipulate. They still had a long way to go before they had a huge bottle. If they moved too slowly or without care, they could wind up with a golf club–shaped object dripping at the end of the pipe.

They went back for another gather. From there it was a building process, putting layer upon layer to form the glass object. As Don Friel, team member and designer of specially built equipment for this world record feat, explained, "Each time, the size of the gather was twice what it was before. When the blowpipe was taken out of the furnace for the sixth time, the gather weighed ninety pounds." It was enough material to make their record-breaking bottle.

That ninety pounds of weight was concentrated at the very tip of the blowpipe. A glassblower's hands have to be at the far end and not to touch the red-hot metal portion of the pipe that has been subjected to the heat of the furnace. Usually this is not a problem, since the weight of the glass is insignificant. But in this case, they needed four men to lift the pipe and a specially designed crossbar attached to the blowpipe to support it and allow them to spin the glass to maintain its shape.

The four team members had to carry this heavy hot load of glass and the blowpipe quickly but carefully to a 4-foot-tall steel drum lined with wooden slats. In smaller glassblowing efforts, the glassblower simply holds the pipe up to his mouth while tilting it upwards and blows. There was no way any one of the four men could sustain that weight, and it would also take a lot of hot air on the part of the blower. The last thing they needed was for one of them to hyperventilate and pass out during this record-breaking attempt. Instead they attached a hose to the blowpipe's neck (the part where the glassblower's lips usually go). The hose rested on a set of steps. Once in place, they immediately began inflating the gather with compressed air.

As the air filled the gather and it began to stretch and grow, a team member using a forklift raised the glassblower. Since glass cools quickly, Tobin and Lewin continuously reheated the glass with torches to keep it pliable. Shintani used special glassblowing tools to lengthen the bottle. When the bottle measured the world record–breaking length, they removed the hose.

But the fun wasn't over yet. They had now designed their bottle, but it was still very fragile and attached to the blowpipe. The blowpipe had to be broken off from the glass, otherwise they'd have the world's largest bottle on a stick. With normal-sized glass, the glassblower would simply score the bottle (make a thin line around the edge, kind of like when you fold a piece of paper back and forth to make a line where it will tear) with a tool called a jack. Then he would simply tap the bottle, and, presto, the glass would break off at the line where the bottle was scored. But this was one big bottle. They had to score it with a file and hit it with a baseball bat. That did the trick.

They now had to work quickly before the thin walls shattered. The bottle had to be shifted from its upright position to a side position. Using a fire-resistant fabric sling, four team members, working like a 911 emergency team with a stretcher, gently placed the bottle and swung it into position while two other team members opened the specially built, extra-large annealing oven door before the bottle could break. They had to keep the bottle in the oven at a certain temperature for a full twenty hours to make sure that after all their efforts, the glass wouldn't break.

Before the Glass Blast weekend was over, the team had set a world record. The glassblowers had worked hard, and it paid off. The event had gone off without a hitch, and they'd created the exact bottle they'd wanted to: a gigantic 7-feet-8-inch-tall clear bottle shaped like one that would hold soda pop. The giant bottle was permanently commemorated in the 1995 *Guinness Book of World Records* and the bottle is now in the museum on permanent display.

Thank goodness none of them had butterfingers!

The First Car Studio
· 1996 ·

Sometimes the craziest ideas lead to a successful venture if you are willing to break the mold and go for it. That's exactly what singer/songwriter/producer Ben Vaughn did with his 1996 album, put out by Rhino Records, called *Rambler '65*. Vaughn has the distinction of recording the first music album ever in an automobile. He turned the backseat of his 1965 Rambler into a recording studio. And this wonderful first for the music industry happened in the driveway of his Collingswood, Camden County, home in New Jersey.

Vaughn's most famous Hollywood success came as composer for the hit NBC television series *3rd Rock from the Sun*. "They were looking for classic American rock 'n' roll as if played by aliens," he said, "and that's what I do naturally so I was a perfect choice."

Vaughn always loved three things: music, Ramblers, and being different. So one day he decided to combine all three.

In 1996 Ben Vaughn had no record deal and no advance money for recording. He was producing some demos for a local group at a studio in Hoboken. One of the members of the group was a conga player who, no matter where they put him in the studio, sounded horrible. The band kept moving him around and put blankets and towels on the walls to get the sound right, but it just wasn't working. Finally, frustrated, Vaughn yelled out, "We should stick him in my car and run a mike out—it's got to sound better than this!" While they didn't do that, a lightbulb lit up in Vaughn's head: "Rock 'n' roll never sounds better than it does on a car radio. Why not record it in a car?"

Musicians from the Beach Boys to Bruce Springsteen have written about their cars, but no one ever actually thought to record in one. Although the idea sounded crazy, Vaughn decided that he may as well try it before someone else got wind of the idea. He didn't want to turn on the radio one day and find out that "U2 would be recording in their limousine."

The only kind of car Vaughn had ever owned since high school was the Rambler. He bought his first Rambler for $200, then another for $300. By 1996 he'd had five Ramblers in all. He felt the car was an underdog, too, with American Motors being an independent company competing against majors like GM and Ford. The combination seemed perfect.

When he got the idea to record in his car, Vaughn owned two Ramblers, a '64 and a '65. He went out to the cars with an acoustic guitar and played a little and recorded a little in both. The music sounded much better in the '65 Rambler—a combination of water leaks and a damp headliner gave just the right touch, an organic sound he was looking for. Then he stomped on the floor of the '65, and the metal vibration sound clinched the deal.

Every morning for the next few days he'd have a cup of coffee, read the paper, and then move his studio from his house out to his car. He didn't skimp on the equipment. He put the recording equipment in the front seat and played the bass guitar and drum machines from the backseat. His amplifier was in the trunk, which became a makeshift isolation booth. Some of the equipment used was an eight-channel mixing board, an eight-track reel to reel, a Casio PT-80, a keyboard/rhythm box, a Casiotone keyboard, a drum machine, a snare drum, a cymbal, a Fender Precision bass, a microphone, an acoustic guitar, a "six-track" synthesizer, pedals, a fuzz machine, an amp, headphones, a receiver, and a turntable. Good thing it was sturdy car!

As was his usual style, he played all the instruments (with the exception of the sitar solo, which was performed by Mike Vogelmann), and he worked without assistance. He had to— there was no room left for anyone else in the car!

Vaughn worked until three o'clock in the afternoon every day, just in time to finish before the neighborhood kids got out of school. A couple of times he missed his deadline, and the kids came up to the window of the car, pressed their noses against it, and asked, "Hey, mister, you making a video for MTV?" Vaughn didn't want to have to explain it because, quite frankly, he wasn't sure why he was doing it himself.

The record was done quickly for one reason: Vaughn was getting claustrophobic in the car with all that equipment. But he was determined to finish the album. Several times he questioned his own sanity. "This is the commitment I had to come up with?," he later commented. He would psyche himself up before every song: "OK, this vocal has got to be it, 'cause I'm going crazy in here." It forced him to do his best performance on the first take. The people in the neighborhood thought he was nuts, but he didn't care.

The first song on the album, "7 Days," was cowritten in five minutes. He said if they'd taken six, he thinks they would have ruined it. He used actual car sounds, like the sound of his foot pounding on the floor, to supplement the music.

A studio on wheels is not always the best for acoustics. So to get the sound he wanted, he had to have the windows rolled up. During one recording session he was singing and playing his guitar pretty loudly, getting into the music. All of a sudden, as he was about to finish another track, he noticed that there were a couple of bees inside the car. They started aiming for his head. The next thing he knew, he was scrambling to get out of the car before he got stung. It wasn't an easy task since he was attached to his equipment. He had his headphones on, and the guitar was plugged into the board. He wound up fleeing the car, dragging everything with him.

It was like a scene from a sitcom.

During another session birds were chirping, sirens were going off, and dogs were barking. You can hear those sounds in the background of that track. Instead of fighting it, Vaughn went with it. A loud airplane flew overhead just as he was about to lay down the track for a song called "The Only Way to Fly." What better way to start it than with a real airplane sound? So he rolled down the window, stuck the microphone outside, and as soon as the plane passed, he started singing.

After he finished recording, he took all the equipment back into the house and mixed the sounds. The experiment was complete. He had no idea that the album would actually be released, but it was and went on to sell well. The album wound up with eleven tracks, and, as a bonus, has a genuine original radio commercial for the 1965 Rambler American. As another twist, as if all this wasn't crazy enough, the cover of the album shows the Rambler with arrows pointing to where each piece of equipment was during the recording.

The total cost to produce this one-of-a-kind New Jersey first was a whopping $48! Who says you have to give an arm and a leg for fame? Sometimes you just need to give up your backseat.

A man, a car, a dream—nothing is impossible or too crazy when you are determined.

A Potpourri of New Jersey Facts

• New Jersey was one of the original thirteen colonies and the third state accepted into the union, on December 18, 1787.

• The state has a total area of 7,836 square miles, of which 315 are covered by water. Only four states are smaller in area.

• New Jersey has 800 lakes and ponds, which are found mostly in the northwest region in the Appalachian Mountains.

• The capital of New Jersey is Trenton.

• The major airport is in Newark, the largest city in the state.

• The nickname for New Jersey is the Garden State because of its many farms that use trucks.

• The state's land masses are more than one billion years old.

• The Lenni-Lenape Indians, an Algonquian tribe, were early inhabitants of New Jersey.

• The population of New Jersey is 8,414,350, according to the 2000 census. The state has the highest population density in America.

• The highest point is High Point, Kittatinny Mountain, at 1,803 feet. The lowest point is 250 feet.

• New Jersey has approximately 120 miles of shoreline.

• The state has over fifty resort towns. Some of the most famous are Asbury Park, Cape May, Atlantic City, Wildwood, and Seaside Heights. Cape May and Long Beach are two of the oldest seaside resorts in the United States.

• It is the largest chemical-producing state in the nation.

• New Jersey has twenty-one counties.

• The state name comes from the island of Jersey in the English Channel. That island had been defended against Parliamentary forces during the English Civil War by one of the colony's original proprietors.

• New Jersey was originally called *Scheyichbi* by the Lenni-Lenape Indians.

• Northern New Jersey is known as the "Embroidery Capital of the World."

• North Jersey has the most shopping malls in one area in the world, with seven major malls in a 25-square-mile radius.

• Two-thirds of the world's eggplants are grown in New Jersey.

• New Jersey has a spoon museum featuring over 5,400 spoons.

• The state is home to the tallest water tower in the world. The 60-foot-tall tower was built in 1961 on Bell Labs property.

•It is home to the Boy Scouts of America headquarters in New Brunswick.

•Leo, the MGM lion, and Elsie, the Borden cow, are both buried in New Jersey. Leo is buried in Morris County and Elsie in Mercer County.

•In 1787 a dark heavy bone was excavated in Woodbury, Gloucester County, and was presented to Benjamin Franklin. Based upon the opinion of a prominent Philadelphia physician, Casper Wistar, Franklin believed the bone was that of a large man. It was a dinosaur bone. (The term "dinosaur" had not even been coined yet.)

•The Baby Ruth candy bar was named after the thirteen-year-old daughter of the only U.S. president from New Jersey, Grover Cleveland. Cleveland was the twenty-second and twenty-fourth president.

•Monobactam, a substance that has the potential to improve antibiotics, was recently discovered in the Pinelands.

•In Franklin, Sussex County, there are over 300 different types of minerals, including the well-known Franklin marble. There is also an open quarry where you can find luminous rocks.

•The first Black man ever to vote did so in New Jersey. His name was Thomas Mundy Peterson, and he voted on March 31, 1870, in a Perth Amboy election to revise the city charter, one day after the Fifteenth Amendment barring race as a factor in voting went into effect. He later became a delegate to the Republican Convention.

•New Jersey is the home of Lena Blackburne's Baseball Rubbing Mud. For over fifty years mud from Pennsauken Creek or near it (the exact location and the owners of the company is a highly guarded secret) has been used by all major-league baseball teams to remove the shine from new baseballs before they are put into play. A single coffee can containing about fifteen pounds of the mud is sent to each team before the start of the season. A can of the mud is on display at the Baseball Hall of Fame.

•Indians roamed freely in Hoboken prior to 1845. They made bowls for their pipes out of stones found there. The Indians named the town *Hoboran-Hackingh,* which means "land of the tobacco pipe."

•Atlantic City is where the street names came from in the original game of *Monopoly.*

•"Little Nipper," the famous black-and-white terrier that promoted RCA Victrola with his head tilted toward a gramophone horn, can be seen in a stained-glass window with four panes created in 1915 for RCA Victor's Camden headquarters.

• Southwestern New Jersey near Vineland is known as the "Cow Capital of the First Frontier." The Cowtown Rodeo has taken place in Woodstown every Saturday night during the summer since 1929 (except during World War II).

•On July 17, 2001, at least fifteen people contacted the police to report seeing golden orange lights moving quietly in a V formation in the New Jersey sky. These lights hovered and then disappeared one at a time, each one fading until they were gone. Some say it was an alien encounter.

•Ben Franklin referred to New Jersey as a "barrel tapped at both ends" because it is linked to two major trade and cultural cities, New York and Philadelphia.

•Parsippany has been named a Tree City USA for twenty-five consecutive years.

•New Jersey has the highest ratio of paved highway to total area.

•The state has the most diners in the world and is sometimes referred to as the "Diner Capital of the World."

•New Jersey is home to the Statue of Liberty and Ellis Island.

•The New Jersey Turnpike and Garden State Parkway are among the safest roads in the United States in terms of accidents per passenger miles.

•The first European to explore New Jersey was Giovanni da Verrazano, a Florentine sailor under the French flag.

•In 1776 the first New Jersey constitution was adopted.

•King's Highway was named by Dutch and English settlers after King Charles. The first street on the left of Town Hall in Middletown is called Penelope Lane, named after Penelope Stout, the "Mother of Middletown."

•Some famous New Jerseyans include: Grover Cleveland, Thomas Edison, Woodrow Wilson, Walt Whitman, Paul Robeson, Norman Mailer, Abbott & Costello, Meryl Streep, Joyce Kilmer, Jack Nicholson, Bruce Springsteen, Jon Bon Jovi, Redman, Das EFX, Naughty by Nature, Sugar Hill Gang, Lords of the Underground, Jason Alexander, Queen Latifah, Shaquille O'Neal, Judy Blume, Aaron Burr, Alexander Hamilton, Whitney Houston, Eddie Money, and Frank Sinatra.

New Jersey Firsts

•The Atlantic City boardwalk is a world-famous landmark. Built in 1870, it was the first boardwalk ever constructed.

•New Jersey was the first state to put *E Pluribus Unum* (from many, one) on a coin. It appeared for the first time on "horse head coppers," which were produced in New Jersey during the 1780s. An act of New Jersey legislation in 1786 enabled three million coins to roll off the press within a two-year period. Three mints were located in Morristown, Elizabethtown, and Rahway. It wasn't until years later that other states followed suit.

•New Jersey invented the traffic circle in 1925, Airport Circle in Camden County. Some things are better left uninvented.

•New Jersey was the first state to use the word "airport," which originated in South Jersey in 1919. One version of the story credits a businessman, Henry Woodhouse, for coining the phrase; in another version the wordsmith is William Dill, an editor for the *Atlantic City Press.*

•The golf tee was first patented by New Jerseyan George Grant in 1899. Grant had two other firsts: He was the first Black dentist and the first Black golfer post Civil War.

•Salt water taffy was first made in Atlantic City in 1883.

• The Seven Stars Tavern in Salem County was the first establishment to have a drive-through window. Back in 1762, a man could ride up on his horse, order a meal, pay, and not have to dismount.

• The first air conditioner was built in Newark in 1911 by Willis Haviland Carrier.

• Bell Labs is famous for many reasons; one is that its team of scientists developed the first transistor in Murray Hill and patented it in 1948.

• Thomas Edison created many firsts from his home in Menlo Park. He devised the phonograph (1877), the first incandescent lightbulb (1879), the commercial film projector (1897), and hundreds of other inventions that are household items today.

• In 1792, Alexander Hamilton formed an investment group called the Society for Establishing Useful Manufactures (S.U.M.) and built Paterson, the nation's first planned industrial city.

• Morristown National Historical Park was the nation's first national park, built in 1933.

• The nation's first Indian reservation, Brotherton, was established August 29, 1758, in Burlington County.

• The Pinelands was the first National Reserve, established in 1979. The Pinelands is home to 39 species of mammal, 299 types of birds, 59 species of reptiles and amphibians, and 91 kinds of fish. Seven of the reptile and amphibian species are only found in the Pinelands.

• New Jersey was home to the first Miss America Pageant, held in Atlantic City in 1921.

•The first time the New Jersey Devils hockey team won the Stanley Cup was in 1995.

New Jersey State Symbols

•State bird is the Eastern goldfinch.

•State fish is the brook trout.

•State seashell is the knobbed whelk *(Busycon carica gmelin)*.

•The state flag is buff-colored with the blue seal of the state in the middle.

•State colors are buff and Jersey blue (decided by Revolutionary War officers).

•State folk dance is the square dance.

•State flower is the common meadow violet.

•State tree is the red oak.

•State animal is the horse.

•State insect is the honeybee *(Apis mellifera)*.

•State tall ship is the *A. J. Meerwald.*

•State motto is "Liberty and Prosperity."

•State demon is the New Jersey Devil. (New Jersey is the only state to have an official state demon.)

•New Jersey has no state song.

Odd New Jersey Laws

•Cabbage can't be sold on Sunday.

•It is against the law to frown at a police officer.

•In Newark it is illegal to sell ice cream after six o'clock in the evening unless the customer has a note from his doctor.

•It is illegal to slurp soup.

•In Trenton it is illegal to throw a bad pickle into the street.

•Anyone who chomps loudly in a restaurant faces penalties.

Bibliography

"Crimes and Punishment." In *The Illustrated Crime Encyclopedia*. Vol. 1. Westport, Conn: Stattman,1994.

Cunningham, John T. *The New Jersey Sampler: Historic Tales of Old New Jersey*. Upper Montclair, N.J.: New Jersey Almanac, 1964.

Dilonno, Mark. *A Guide to New Jersey's Revolutionary War*. Piscataway, N.J. and London: Rutgers University Press, 2000.

Encyclopedia Americana. Volume 14, pp. 522–523. Danbury, Conn., Grolier, 1996.

Fernicila, Richard G. *Twelve Days of Terror: A Definitive Investigation of the 1916 New Jersey Shark Attacks*. Guilford, Conn.: Lyons Press, 2001.

Fleming, Thomas. *New Jersey: A History*. New York: W.W. Norton & Company, 1984.

Getz, William. *Sam Patch: Ballad of a Jumping Man*. New York: Franklin Watts, 1986.

Hopp, Julius. "Voice-Broadcasting the Stirring Progress of the 'Battle of the Century.'" *Wireless Age* (August 1921).

Majoor, Mireille. *Inside the Hindenburg*. New York: Madison Press, 2000.

Murphy, Jim. *Blizzard*. New York: Scholastic Press, 2000.

Putnam, Peter Brock. *Love in the Lead: The Miracle of the Seeing Eye Dog*. New York: University Press of America, 1997.

Roberts, Russell. *Discover the Hidden New Jersey*. New Jersey: Rutgers University Press, 1995.

Royle, John, and Sons. "Sam Patch—The Jersey Jumper." *The Royal Forum,* no. 144 (September 15, 1973).

Seymour, Harold. *Baseball: The Early Years.* New York: Oxford University Press, 1960.

Stockton, Frank R. *Stories of New Jersey.* Piscataway, N.J.: Rutgers University Press, 1987.

Vogt, L. A. "Morristown Ghost." A pamphlet published in 1792.

"War of the Worlds," *Trenton Evening Times*, October 21, 1938.

Witcover, Jules. *Sabotage at Black Tom: Imperial Germany's Secret War in America, 1914–1917.* Chapel Hill, N.C.: Algonquin Books, 1989.

Internet Sources

www.levins.com/creature.html
www.ahherald.com
www.dupont.com/teflon
www.johnhoneyman.com
www.weirdnj.com

Travel Information

Edison National Historic Site
Main Street and Lakeside
Avenue
West Orange, NJ 07052
(973) 736–0550, ext. 42

Hadrosaurus replica
Philadelphia Academy of
Natural Sciences
1900 Benjamin Franklin
Parkway
Philadelphia, PA 19103
(215) 299–1000
www.acnatsci.org

Half Moon replica
The New Netherlands
Museum and Half Moon
Visitor's Center
P.O. Box 10609
Albany, NY 12201–5609
(518) 443–1609 (Main)
www.newnetherland.org

Lucy the Margate Elephant
8200 Altantic Avenue
Margate, NJ 08402
(609) 823–6473
www.lucytheelephant.org

New Jersey Historical Society
52 Park Place
Newark, NJ 07102
(973) 596–8500, ext. 248
www.jerseyhistory.org

The Seeing Eye (by appoint-
ment only)
P.O. Box 375
Morristown, NJ 07963
(973) 539–4425
www.theseeingeye.org

World's Tallest Glass Bottle
Wheaton Village
1501 Glasstown Road
Millville, NJ 08332
(856) 825–6800 or (800)
998–4552
www.wheatonvillage.org

Index

About the Author

Fran Capo is a stand-up comic, adventurer, motivational speaker, voice-over artist, certified hypnotherapist, freelance writer with over 300 published articles, and has the distinction of being the *Guinness Book of World Records* Fastest Talking Female clocked at 603.32 words per minute. She has been featured on over 1,000 radio and 250 television shows including: *Ripley's Believe it or Not, Total Request Live, The Late Show, Entertainment Tonight, The Weakest Link,* and *Larry King Live.* She is the cocreator of the three-time award-winning cybersitcom *The Estrogen Files: Money, Men and Motherhood.* As a six-time author her books include: Globe Pequot's *It Happened in New York* and her novel, *Almost a Wise Guy.*

Fran has a passion for life; her motto is "Fear nothing." She has walked on hot coals, bungee jumped, scuba dived with sharks, flown combat aircraft, and driven racecars. Fran is a single mom, a Queens College graduate, and lives in Howard Beach, New York. To learn more about Fran or to have her speak for your organization, you can go to her Web site, www.francapo.com.